AI Game Changers: Revolutionizing Sports Training for Young Athletes

*It gives us great excitement and enthusiasm to present **"AI Game Changers: Revolutionizing Sports Training for Young Athletes"***

AI Game Changers uses Artificial Intelligence, Game Theory and Gaming Elements to provide effective personalised sports training for young athletes, a novel research effort to bring the power of artificial intelligence to sports training. This book is authored by DR. Selva, AI Robotics Strategist & Visionary Author and a specialist in AI in Information technology, and Vijay Sellayah, an athlete himself and a coach of young cricketers. Together, and with contributions from some twelve other sportsmen/ sportswomen from other fields of sport, they bring a unique combination of expertise and experience between the field of sciences and that of practical sports.

Selva Sugunendran & Vijay Sellayah

Hello & Welcome!

If you have been looking at the title of the book, let me say, any of the following titles would apply to the contents of this book:

BOOK TITLES:

Six compelling titles for your book that will appeal specifically to the young athlete on Amazon:

1. "AI Game Changers: Revolutionizing Sports Training for Young Athletes"

2. "Future Athletes: Mastering Sports with AI-Powered Training"

3. "Sporting Edge: Harnessing AI to Elevate Your Game"

4. "Next-Gen Athletes: Achieving Excellence with AI"

5. "AI in Sports: The Ultimate Guide for Young Athletes"

6. "Peak Performance: How AI is Transforming Sports Training"

All these titles emphasise the radical newness of the technologies associated with AI, the prime focus on sporting coaches looking to optimise their training practices, and the allure of perfection and optimal performance – all of which might seem attractive to young athletes who are keen to improve their sporting skills and performance.

ABOUT THE BOOK

It gives us great excitement and enthusiasm to present **"AI Game Changers: Revolutionizing Sports Training for Young Athletes"**

AI Game Changers uses Artificial Intelligence, Game Theory and Gaming Elements to provide effective personalised sports training for young athletes, a novel research effort to bring the power of artificial intelligence to sports training. This book is authored by DR. Selva, a specialist in AI applications in Information technology, and Vijay Sellayah, a cricket coach of young athletes. Together, and with contributions from some twelve other sportsmen/ sportswomen from other fields of sport, they bring a unique combination of expertise and experience between the field of sciences and that of practical sports.

There's been a long and wild crossover between sport and technology, starting with the unpredictable autonomy of the squash ball and speeding up with the unpredictability of the modern world. With AI, something entirely new is happening. What was once a mere intersection of interests is becoming a new performance synergy that will transform sport and the way athletes train, improve and play. AI Game Changers is not so much a manual as it is a manifesto, a declaration of a new era of sport, an era where data and numbers, machine and game, will become just as fundamental as muscle and motive.

The expertise of Dr Selva, who is highly qualified in Information Technology, AI and Robotics, also ensures that the concepts treated in the book are current and scientifically sound. Through DR Selva's lens, the technology behind AI is demystified, at the same time making it more readable and more exciting. As someone who has his fingers on the pulse of the latest advancements in this field, DR Selva offers very valuable insights to the reader by sketching for them training tips & performance hacks! A very important aspect of Dr Selva's vision was the democratisation of AI technologies. He wanted to give the task of training a human body to the tools that so far were used exclusively by high-budget research labs and high-profitable professional teams.

Vijay Sellayah pursued sports throughout his life and now teaches cricket by being a coach of the youngsters in cricket. It is important to say that the name Sellayah is synonymous with sports. His late father Walter Sellayah was a great sportsman and so were Vijay's elder brothers Mahesa and Selvendran whose athletic achievements were very well known in their young days.

Collectively, this book lays out a persuasive vision for the future of sports training, in which artificial intelligence smartly supplements the drills and guidance of sports' living wisdom, empowering kids not to lean, but to leap; to use AI not as a crutch but as a catapult.

The Purpose of This Book

In that respect, the book's authors have a clear second agenda. "Our primary purpose … is to educate - First, we want to educate the players who are in the pipeline so that they understand how broad, and how far [AI in Sports] can go". The book outlines the reasons why sportsmen and women will need to embrace AI as a part of their primary training regime.

For humans, the guidance is even more urgent to provide since, as of now, a Grand Tour cyclist cannot bike a 2,000-mile Tour de France route while sleeping, but perhaps this is only because we've not thought to design and build systems that help us do this. Second, this book is aspirational. It is written to be seen, and hopefully read, by athletes when they're young so that the possibility of using technology to enhance their training regimes gets lodged early in their imaginations. Each page is meant to push young athletes' imaginations to think: 'Could I do it like that with this extra tool?' When it comes to young athletes reading this book, they are twice blessed by the technology adoption discussion: they grow up with technology being a natural part of their lives, and they are encouraged from an early age to imagine what life might look like if they had access to various technological enhancements. Yes, athletes would need to perfect the use of AI-enhanced training tools, but they also need to perfect other ordinary tasks related to athletic training that, while mostly mundane, can also become part of their regular lives and routines.

The Journey Ahead

Over the coming pages, you'll travel from field to field at the intersection of sports and AI, witnessing how data can be harnessed to craft tailor-made training to fit everyone, how machine learning algorithms can help predict and prevent injuries, and how virtual reality can simulate the competition itself to prepare for it.

But you'll also find stories of resistance, observations about the psychology of training, and reflections on the human nature of coaching. This book is not about how AI is changing sport, but how the changing landscape of sport is changing everyone involved – how athletes train, how they think, how they compete.

A Call to Action

To the athletes of the future, the teenagers who will pick up this book: we challenge you to view AI as an athlete's best friend when it comes to helping you achieve the highest standard possible. Work with the technologies that will enhance your training and broaden your mental spaces. Sports of tomorrow will be those whose work is characterised by a marriage of human talent and training with technology; you have joined the party of resurrection.

To the coaches, parents and mentors: encourage your athletes to investigate these new opportunities; be inquisitive, be cynical, but most of all be informed. These tools and technologies could potentially revolutionise performance in training sports, but they need enquiring minds and open hearts to do so.

But 'AI Game Changers' is far more than just a vision of the human future of sports. It's a tribute to the profound desire for human knowledge – and the ingenuity of mankind, and of the athletes, creators and champions whose careers we've met along the way, to now conquer uncharted territory with the help of AI that will, in turn, create a game for people that's better than any we've managed to create so far. Come. Let us play.

"Welcome to the future. Welcome to "AI Game Changers."

PS. For those, who are totally new to AI and wish to learn more about AI, you could read DR. Selva's other books on AI, starting with "AI for Beginners", "Mastering the Mind of Machines", "Rogue AI- The Oppenheimer Moment" ,"AI Trilogy" and "AI and its Trajectory – Navigating The Age of Enlightenment and addressing the threat to humanity" These books are all available on Amazon.

However, the current book can be read, understood and implemented without additional information.

INTRODUCTION TO THE BOOK

Welcome to a new training world: Welcome to **"AI Game Changers: Transforming Sports Training for Young Athletes"**, a revolutionary book about artificial intelligence (AI) to help you train the athlete in you with future-forward insights, strategies and tips. This book is not simply about informing you about the future; it is about changing how you train, play and develop in sports today. It is for you, the high-school player who has big dreams for your life and your playing career; the collegiate player who wants to make it to the next level; and it's for the coach who wants to update his or her training programme. It's for you! Not only will this book help you avoid common mistakes, but you'll also learn how to focus your attention to succeed with AI that can provide exceptional performance feedback, game analysis and more.

No longer merely a sci-fi buzzword, AI is here and tangible, altering the future in industries everywhere, including sport. The timely use of AI by young athletes marks the transition point from good to great, from winning to triumphing. The applications range from optimising physical conditioning and techniques to shaping mental battles and preventing injuries, all tools that can elevate a young athlete in the sporting arena.

We wrote this book to fill this gap, to explore the power of state-of-the-art AI technologies applied to training, to offer a glimpse of the landscape of applications for players and coaches, including machine learning to design personalised training programmes on the fly, and generated realities to train in immersive virtual environments that mimic the real-world reality of the stadium. Each chapter of this book presents a technology in an accessible way to help you navigate from the theoretical background to the practical application.

Why AI and Why Now?

Sports across the world are changing faster than ever, as advances in technology help athletes supersede previous records. In this picture, AI can fuel this progress by bringing the precision of training, insights from data that the team's coach would miss, and health data that helps you to perform your best today without sacrificing tomorrow's health or career.

Young athletes catching a glimpse of the AI-assisted training available to athletes of the future achieve three goals. First, working with present-day AI learns you how to cope with ultra-hi-tech ultra-medical ultra-sports environments of tomorrow. Second and most importantly perhaps, AI-assisted training allows you to glean the maximum value out of your training time. Thirdly it guides you to go further and higher in your sports performance without taking unnecessary risks to your energy, your health and life. You will train bravely but resourcefully. My book introduces these ideas to you, its readers. It starts with sport-AI basics and sport-AI textbooks, then sketches sport-AI in individual sports disciplines, and ends with sport-AI trends and ethics.

Your Pathway Through the Book

Unless otherwise noted, each of Parts I and II concerns the interface of AI with individual sport, examining how AI is used to analyse and optimise fundamental tactics in cricket, football and track events, from the bowling actions of cricket to the mechanics of the sprints on a track.

Part III to XI discuss employing AI into team tactics and game-day strategies and provide information on how AI tools analyse the game footage to develop winning strategies in sports such as Rugby, Tennis, Hockey,

Baseball, Basketball Volleyball, Football and Golf.

PART XII examines how AI can be used to regiment more training across the sporting landscape, not just for strength and conditioning, but injury prevention and recovery, all areas that can dramatically increase your chances of longevity in your sport, to allow for a longer career and keep you in the best shape possible to recover more rapidly from injury.

Part XIII concludes our 'futuristic' look at the developments in AI for sports; and allows for a more sobering reality check on the ethical ramifications of introducing AI in the training of our young athlete 'in-waiting'.

The book is sprinkled with practical examples and real-world data, to ensure that you do not just learn some mathematical theory – you can start applying it right away. The goal of this book is to demystify AI in sports training. By bringing it down to the level of sports training – of the 'doing'; of throwing a disc, spiking a ball or swinging a golf club, which is a unique method. The mathematics within this book is entirely learning-based, as opposed to performance-based. Mathematical formulas and performance classes do not exist; instead, the system learns directly from experiencing the games and tournaments being played.

Beyond the Game

One last thing, as you navigate this journey with the book at hand, keep in mind that mastering AI in sports involves not just exploiting technology but also a truly mindset developed for learning and adaptation. The technology of sport is changing rapidly, and keeping up with cutting-edge tools and methodologies will often determine the difference between success and failure.

AI Game Changers: Revolutionizing Sports Training for Young Athletes is a book that not only guides you in your sports training, but motivates you to explore new ways of thinking, to train smarter, and to be open to the possibilities that AI can provide for you.

Put on your shoes. Ready, Set, Go!

TABLE OF CONTENTS

Each chapter could serve as a guide for a budding sportsman, describing all the conceivable ways young athletes could use AI to enhance their performance.

INTRODUCTION TO AI IN SPORTS:

CHAPTER ONE

Introduction to AI in Sports Coaching

1.1: Understanding the Role of AI in Modern Sports Training

While experts in artificial intelligence are hard at work creating virtual assistants that speak human-sounding sentences and react to human emotions, other AI experts are finding the influence of the artificial mind practically useful in different areas. Notably, sports coaching is just one area that has greatly benefited from artificial intelligence.

Given the exponential growth of AI technology, the importance of AI in sports coaching will be even more significant than ever, and this chapter reviews the increasing importance of such a phenomenon. Sport coaching not only leads athletes to win, but also plays a vital role in enhancing psychological, physical, and mental health of people. Thus, this chapter explores the importance of AI in sports coaching, and examines the pervasive influence of AI in this field and its contribution from different perspectives.

Algorithms, machine learning, data analytics … artificial intelligence (AI) has entered the sporting lexicon. In athletics, AI can augment coaching by optimising training regimes, or aid decision-making on the pitch. There are AI training systems for NBA players and Predictive Analytics in cornering for Formula One cars. A sports car can remember each corner it takes and, by selecting the best line in terms of its fastest lap, pilot the driver through it. Closer to the top of the game, the launch plans for a space mission are refined by a computer, and cruise control enables pilots to fly those missions safely. On a small scale, AI serves as a co-pilot for tests flown by student pilots; on the larger scale, it guides the massive rocket for separation and landing in the Pacific Ocean. This technology can also be used to play sports, improving decision-making, bringing real-time intelligence, enhancing performance, and amplifying entertainment. At CruFrance.com, AI uses data to reduce the risk of injury in sport.

1.2: Historical Evolution and Current Trends

AI's ascent in sports started with the basic data analytics tools that coaches and analysts came to employ in their analysis of players and game-plans. Early-stage analytics tools ranged from simple statistical methods to video analysis tools where coaches could break down game film and mini-clips to show improvement areas. Early-stage analytics also involved things like shot charts and split-second decision calculators. With the proliferation of such tools came an increase in sophistication, which has led to more complex AI applications today.

One of the first highly visible examples of AI in sport was replay video analysis software that allowed coaches to freeze frame by frame the action on the pitch. Software such as Dartfish and Hudl in the late 1990s provided detailed breakdowns of player movements, techniques and tactics. They helped to lay the foundation for the array of more sophisticated AI applications that have since become ubiquitous in sport, including machine learning algorithms that predict player performance and risk of injury.

Now, AI in sports involves everything from wearable technology to biomechanical analysis to predictive analytics to virtual reality training. Sensors in wearable devices collect information about an athlete's body in real time, like heart rate, speed and movement, and are analysed using artificial intelligence algorithms to give real-time, personalised training feedback and tracking.

Applied to cricket, AI can help identify patterns in a bowler's action, suggesting tweaks to improve consistency and line. The ball's trajectory, pace and spin are key, as would be any variations that affect their standings or other elements. Football, too, has seen AI analysing player movement and positional shifts that can improve scoring – or stopping it.

And AI is starting to play into mental toughness, which is another important factor in athletic success. It can involve employing neurofeedback and cognitive training – both powered by AI – to help an athlete improve concentration, resilience and on-the-go decision-making.

1.3: Benefits of AI in Sports Coaching

1.3.1. Enhanced Analysis:
Aided by greater predictive computerised data, AI can provide your sports coach with more in-depth and accurate performance data analysis than ever before. This means that training programmes and fitness sessions will be honed towards the very specific strengths and weaknesses of the individual athlete.

1.3. 2: Injury Prevention and Management:
When an athlete's movement patterns are captured and analysed by AI, the system can predict the likelihood of injury, and recommend preventive protocols for the athlete to avoid the possibility of injury and enhance post-injury rehabilitation while also improving the healing process.

1.3.3: Maximised training regimes:

Machine learning algorithms can process more data than a human brain. This means an AI can calculate more options and factors to develop the most effective training regime, potentially giving athletes the edge by providing optimal loading, rest and exercise variations that most effectively enhance performance.

1.3.4: Game Plan:

AI analytics can dismantle the opponent's strategies and identify his vulnerabilities. This information is very helpful in creating game plans and tactics that could exploit the opponent's weaknesses.

1.3. 5: Mental conditioning:

biofeedback, cognitive training and other AI techniques help athletes improve their mental strength and focus when competing. Mental sharpness in peak performance is crucial in high-pressure situations, where mental toughness can make the difference between winning and losing.

1.4: Challenges and Ethical Considerations

Even if AI can facilitate best practices in sports, using it could create legal, ethical and financial problems. Who will have access to the data? What measures will safeguard the huge amounts of data involved from being stolen or misused? If success is increasingly determined by AI, it could create a situation of over-reliance on technology. AI might have a use in augmenting human expertise, but it clearly can't replace it.

1.5: Conclusion

The application of AI to the world of sports coaching will mark a new era of how athletes prepare, compete and succeed. From the use of data analytics, machine learning and algorithms, coaches and athletes can unlock new potentials in the sporting realm. As technology continues to progress, with every iteration bringing more and more possibilities, the applications of AI in sports are boundless, and the future looks promising as we will soon be witnessing athletes achieve feats of human superiority with more clarity and precision than ever known before.

PART-TWO

AI IN CRICKET BOWLING: PRECISION AND CONSISTENCY

CHAPTER TWO

AI in Cricket Bowling: Precision and Consistency

2.1: Techniques to Improve Line and Length

If the line is not accurate, there'll be too many extras. But there is another factor. The off or leg stump – and, by extension, wide-slips and fine-slips – present moving targets for the bowler. Staying online and maintaining good length are crucial to cricketers. For decades, bowlers have had to rely on feel and intuition to control their line and length. But there's a new twist in this centuries-old procedural occupation. Artificial intelligence (AI) has become more involved in delivering improvements in the accuracy of line and length. For the bowler, this means data-driven advice and training regimens are now available on their smartphone.

AI-powered video analysis systems have become an important tool in the bowler's arsenal. Film of bowlers in action throughout practice and in a game, can be captured shot by shot in high definition. An AI system can analyse the film frame-by-frame as a bowler repeats an action over a period. For example, these systems can pinpoint differences in line and length that can arise from subtle arm angle, wrist position and follow-through inconsistencies, uncovering details that may be difficult for the bowler's eye to recognise. With the help of AI, coaches can provide the bowler with tailored feedback and corrective measures to build a mechanical repeatable action for more consistent success.

Further, incorporating virtual batsmen into these simulations can enable bowlers to practise playing against various pitch conditions and batting tendencies. And bowlers can hone their performance by varying their deliveries, using the simulations to adapt to the constellation of selectors working against them. Of course, it's not just AI bowlers and simulated wickets that can exploit the power of machine learning. AI can also enable the development of virtual coaching assistants: mental 'ghosts' that track a bowler's performance during practice sessions and mete out real-time advice. Drop an AI-controlled sensor under the bowler's arm and into the ball – a 'hawk-eye of the arm' – and a virtual assistant could use the data it gathers to offer real-time advice on how to tweak one's technique so that a delivery finds its ideal rhythm and, in theory, catches the edge of the bat often.

2.2: Spin, Swing, and Speed Optimization Using AI

The realisation of all this can be helpful rather than counterproductive to cricket bowling, not only for the purposes of improving line and length (so much for the novelty of AI). It can also work to optimise spin, swing and the level of speed a bowler achieves, all of which can be major factors and powers of influence in achieving success and victory in the game.

2.2.1: Spin Optimization:

Spin bowling has always been an area of intense focus for researchers in the field of motions sports. Spinners have to apply the right forces to the ball in order to get it to spin. AI systems extract features of spin – the number of revolutions per minute (RPM) and the axis of rotation – and improve them. If the ball is rotating around, say, an axis perpendicular to its direction of travel, it will tend to spin off the pitch and break away from the batsman. On the other hand, if the axis is parallel, the revolutions will tug the ball along, inducing a large amount of sideways spin. The toss can be determined with a new system where a speeding bowling ball is gripped firmly between the thumb of the bowler and the fingers of the umpire By analysing the spinner's grip, finger placement and release, AI systems 'coach' the player to generate more spin. For example, AI can figure out if the spinner needs to produce a greater top spin or back spin, and how to place the fingers on the seam to achieve it.

Further, AI could deliver precision models of atmospheric conditions and how they affect spin. For example, spinners could estimate how a new ball would interact with different surfaces, and how bowling techniques could be adjusted to extract optimal spin under certain atmospheric conditions. As a result, a bowler might opt to use different amounts of spin under different conditions to achieve a desired outcome.

2.2.2: Swing Optimization:

Data from high-speed cameras and remote sensors reveal that swing bowling is largely driven by the aerodynamics of moving the ball through the atmosphere unpredictably. Until well into the 20th century, swing bowling depended more on fitted seam, wrist angle, release point and follow-through, but today AI can detect these variations and provide re-al-time data on how they are linked to across-the-seam and off-the-seam movement, as well as 'reverse-swing' movement, called back spin. AI now plays an increasingly important role in tracking, training and boost-ing skills through the accurate reporting of data that helps bowlers to achieve optimal effects.

Awareness of atmospheric conditions that affect swing is another area where AI is essential, as humidity, wind speed and temperature can all impact a ball's flight. AI algorithms, analysing live weather data, can advise bowlers on how to adapt their approach to exploit the swing possibilities on that day.

2.2.3: Speed Optimization:

A fast bowler delivers the ball with speed, accuracy and organisational control. Thanks to AI-equipped wearable devices, the biomechanical components of his run-up, arm speed and follow-through are tracked during a delivery. Analysing those data helps to pinpoint what needs alteration to reach the desired speed without loss of accuracy.

For one, by evaluating players' technique based on biomechanics, AI can monitor the physical and mental profile of a bowler's performance; fatigue levels can thus be tracked, enabling AI to advise on optimal rest durations to avoid physical injury and loss in form. In the mental domain, AI can also make bowlers more resilient by creating simulations of high-octane bowling situations to mentally toughen players and equip them with techniques to withstand pressure.

2.3: Case Studies and Real-World Applications

Many cricket clubs and academies too have embraced AI technologies in their training programmes with great success. The use of AI-powered video analysis has been instrumental in the Indian Premier League (IPL) cricket franchises assessing and improving their delivery skillset, especially for bowlers. These tools do a parallel analysis on footage from match videos and practice sessions, helping build a template on technique and identifying deviations to improve performance and consistency.

Cricket's Australian teams, too, have been 'cheating' by using AI to identify the weaknesses of batsmen that their opponents target. These bowling plans are developed using data collected by AI algorithms on their usual playing styles. 68 Three-Life: A Project (2016) Democracies that do not want to be more vulnerable than others will have to use big data, too.

2.4: Future Directions and Innovations

Moving forward, the potential applications for AI in cricket bowling appear to be rich. New technologies are likely to mean improvements in AI tools too, particularly with machine learning, deep learning etc becoming more mainstream. These technologies can process large amounts of data and identify complex trends not previously recognisable.

An obvious area of development is to use such systems to detect in advance the possibility of injuries. One can then monitor the 'at-risk' bowler more closely, for example by measuring the workload every time they bowl and give corrective feedback before the situation turns serious. Ubiquitous systems built into the cricket gear worn by the fast bowlers could be a real game-changer. As we all know, the fast bowlers run the biggest physical risks. That's where we really need to focus our attention to keep them in the game longer.

A third promising area is pairing AI with virtual reality (VR) training where learners can practise bowling under simulated match conditions in game-environment scenarios. Such a system, complemented with AI analytics, could offer a realistic yet controlled training ground.

2.5: Conclusion

The technology has allowed cricket bowlers to attain previously unimaginable levels of accuracy and consistency. By using algorithm to model the ball's flight and incorporating machine-learning techniques to determine relevant parameters, the app can advise a bowler on issues of the line of attack, length and direction of swing (in the case of spin bowlers), the amount of spin added to the ball, and the speed with which to deliver the delivery. CricViz will show cricket bowlers how to improve their line and length more effectively and efficiently Incorporating AI into the training of cricketers may be useful not only for individual bowlers in achieving an optimal line and length, spin and swing, and speed, but also for improving the strategic richness of cricket activity. There is no limit to what the use of AI might achieve once it comes to cricket in the near, or even more distant, future.

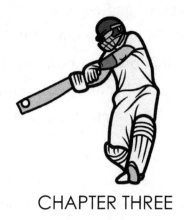

CHAPTER THREE

Enhancing Batting Skills with AI

3.1: Shot Selection and Timing

In cricket, batting is a complex skill that combines hand-eye coordination with tactical canniness and mental fortitude. Crucial batting skills include shot selection and timing: two 'human' choices. Traditionally, these batting skills are honed through thousands of hours of practice and in-game experience. Artificial intelligence (AI) is ushering in new ways of improving these batting skills, with a host of data-driven insights and training techniques.

Batsmen are now able to make decisions about shot selection with the help of AI systems because these artificially intelligent technologies can analyse large amounts of data like match footage from thousands of matches, gameplay from practice sessions, and games in real time, and then provide feedback to batsmen. Using that data, it can assess a batsman's shot selection and suggest improvements and even optimal shot selections in various situations.

Playing to a batsman's weaknesses by bowling only or mostly certain types of deliveries is one of the handiest tools for captains and battle-wise bowlers. AI assists batsmen in figuring out what their weaknesses are by creating different match situations and bowling various types of deliveries, seeing how the batsman handles them and finding the patterns. Armed with that knowledge, batsmen can then make better educated reactions during games.

The other important batting element is timing. Here is where AI can provide immediate feedback on the optimal split-second of a batsman's swing before the ball reaches the bat. Sensors and high-speed cameras, working in tandem, detect the most subtle of movements, from the batsman's stance to his back lift and follow-through. By charting the information from these movements, the AI can pinpoint where the batsman should start his stroke for optimal timing. This feedback helps shape technique. It's easy to spot if the bat didn't connect with the ball at the right moment and the ball is resulting in a weak, uppish stroke.

In addition, physiological monitoring provided by AI-powered wearable devices assist a batsman with maintaining health, by keeping track of his heart rate and muscular motions, providing information related to his physiological readiness and fatigue. This information linked with a batsman's batting performance can help AI inform) a batsman about modifications he should make to his training regime to improve (improve his timing and reduce his injury risk.

3.2: Analysing Opponents' Bowling Patterns

Reading the ball from a bowler's grip and predicting their line and length is fundamental to batting, but arguably more important is understanding a bowler's tactics, their approaches, strengths and weaknesses. An AI could use vast amounts of data on each bowler to provide a batsman with insight on their opponents. Advanced analysis could enable batsmen to devise more targeted strategies to good effect.

Historical data encompassing the performance output of a bowler over a vast number of deliveries becomes input for an AI system designed to learn. The first-degree inputs can be variables linked to the type of delivery used (e.g., swing, off-spin, etc), speeds of delivery, line and length, and way the same deliveries are used in different match situations, for instance the ninth over in a T20 (20-over) match compared with the 49th over of a 50-over match. Using what AI experts call 'pattern extraction' (simply put, 'finding the common patterns within large amounts of data'), the algorithms seek out trends and variables that might predict the likelihood of a given delivery variety to be employed in such a context. The batsman knows what kind of delivery to expect based on probability of encountering a given type of delivery in this match situation.

For example, it could break down an adjustment that a bowler makes in a powerplay, middle overs and death over, to prep the batsman to spot the phases of the innings in which the bowler may be more prone to making an adjustment that can be exploited. Say a bowler is more likely to bowl a greater percentage of slower balls during the death overs. Now the batsman might march out to bat knowing to 'go big or go home' or clamber into the nets and discuss where they want to be to help play out the bowler's strengths – a short fine leg or fine leg to create space to play a scoop.

But the AI also analyses team strategies and field placements – where the fielder is on the field – to help devise the optimal 'shot placement' (i.e., where to hit the ball) and maximise the scoring opportunities available. This strategic insight helps the batsmen make better decisions and exploit the gaps in the field.

Secondly, AI's capacity to perform live provides feedback to the batsmen as and when the game takes place. Wearable devices and smarter bats fitted with sensors can send information to the AI, which in turn provides real-time feedback to the batsman. For instance, if a bowler bowls with a particular grip or the delivery unfolds at a specific release spot, AI can suggest the best response, based on its analysis of a similar delivery.

Some cricket teams and individual players have already begun using AI in training sessions to good effect. International teams such as Australia and England employ AI-assisted tools to research opponents in advance of tournaments so that the batsmen are ready for diverse bowling attacks. They use AI to help players identify footage and statistics of bowlers from other countries so they can practise facing virtual versions of them.

Though the AI currently remains strictly behind the scenes, at the level of the individual cricketer professional batsmen and bowlers already practise simulators modelled upon real match conditions. By deploying AI, cricketers get the benefit of wider, more realistic match scenarios and the opportunity to pit themselves against virtual 'ghosts' of the world's leading quick and spin bowlers. Through immediate feedback and responsive adjustments via AI analysis of their own technique, batsmen and bowlers can fine-tune shot selection and timing in ways that were previously far less effective.

3.3: Conclusion

In addition, over-the-top use of artificial intelligence will also help batsmen polish their skills and master the art of shot selection and timing and analysing the pattern of the opposition bowlers or throwers. Statistical data analysis, motion capture and predictive models will help a batsman get deeper insights into the game. The information collated will then be leveraged to guide batsmen so that they can play better and smarter. AI-driven tools will help players enhance their technical skills as well as develop newer ways of making tactical and strategic decisions on the pitch. This makes cricket an excellent candidate for further use cases of AI technology.

CHAPTER FOUR

Fielding Excellence: AI Techniques for Perfecting Skills

4.1: Reaction Time Improvement

Think of cricket. Fielding is a core component of the game, and a great deal of the match's outcome might be influenced by how well the fielders react to the flight of the ball and position themselves to try and stop the run or take a vital catch. For decades, fielding has been learned through lengthy practice under pressure, but AI techniques are beginning to complement these skills. In a similar way, AI is now being used to improve players' reaction times and positioning, while enhancing accuracy in catching crucial balls that dash towards the players at speed.

Reaction time is a key component of good fielding. All things being equal, a faster reaction time will result in a better ground ball play. AI technologies can aid fielders by tracking their movement and reflexes, detecting areas of improvement for better reactions.

The most used tool in this regard is artificial intelligence (AI)-driven motion capture systems, which comprise a series of high-speed cameras and sensors and use detailed digital reproductions of the player to recreate the lower body motion of the fielder in real time. The systems have a series of data points about a fielder's movement that can analyse the speed of their reactions when playing against different types of balls and can also highlight areas for offline correction. For example, AI might suggest that a slight change in the ball's trajectory would have led to a much better initial response from the fielder to glove a ball, owing to the latter's incorrect distribution of weight or his/her wrong posture.

Furthermore, artificial-intelligence-enhanced, virtual-reality training environments allow fielders to practise their responses to play scenarios from the field, helping them to be better prepared for specific situations during a match. AI-powered VR allows fielders to practise high-catch play, ground balls as well as close-in fielding, by serving up these scenarios in virtual environments. Based on the fielder's performance, the complexities of the play scenarios are modulated to aid in learning and problem-solving.

A third area where AI is being used to boost reaction times are via predictive analytics techniques. By crunching masses of historical data on a fielder's performance, AI can predict which weaknesses the fielder might suffer from and recommend tailor-made exercises to improve reaction times. For example, if data reveals that a fielder suffers from a recurrent inability to respond to incoming ballets hitting the left side of his body, AI could recommend drills to strengthen that area.

4.2: Positioning and Catching Accuracy

And, beyond reaction times, AI could be applied to improve fielder placement and catching skills. A fielder's positioning is considered optimal when it allows the fielder to cover as much ground as possible and be in the right spot at the right time. AI techniques help to compute optimal fielder placements as a function of game situations and the assumed tendencies of the opposing batters.

One method is making use of AI's capacity for intelligent manipulation of heat maps and spatial analysis. By scanning enormous amounts of data on previous trajectories of balls hit by different types of batsmen in various contexts of the game, heat maps can be generated on those areas into which the ball might well be hit. Fielders and coaches can benefit by placing themselves at the locations suggested by such maps. For example, if a batsman has played many of his shots in the region near the cover, a few fielders can be placed in that region so that there is some likelihood of the ball being intercepted.

Catching accuracy can also be improved through AI, and this is done by analysing the biomechanics of a fielder's catching technique. It is common for us to analyse the biomechanics of the catching and batting techniques of sportspersons using high can pick up on subtle differences such as the fielder's hands not being in a good position or having slightly different timing. Based on these insights, AI can recommend corrective actions and specific techniques that can improve catching accuracy.

Furthermore, AI-powered wearable devices, such as smart gloves, can offer feedback to catchers and fielders as they rehearse their techniques in practice sessions. These devices have sensors embedded in them and track the movement of the fielder's hands and the grip. As the fielder goes to catch a ball, the AI system analyses the data to evaluate different aspects of the catching attempt such as the placement of the hands and firmness of the grip. The system then gives the fielder instant feedback on techniques that need improvement. Feedback along with rehearsal practice will surely help improve the fielder's play.

AI can also help make fielding drills more effective by providing adaptive training. Adaptive training programmes would use data from previous training sessions to adjust the difficulty and content of drills according to the fielder's level of learning. For example, if a fielder has mastered basic catching techniques – in terms of practicing catches at certain speeds and angles – the AI system can advance the challenge an appropriate amount by practising catches with a wider variety of speeds and angles in its fielding work outs.

4.3: Case Studies and Real-World Applications

Several cricket teams and academies already use AI to provide fielding training, with good results. For instance, the Indian cricket team has begun using AI-driven analysis to boost their strength and efficacy in fielding. By looking at prior playing patterns of opponents' batting and fielding positions, teams can use AI to boost fielding efficiency and reduce 'gully' (missed catches).

Similarly, the England cricket team has used AI to inform their fielding drills and improve reaction times. Through their use of AI-powered VR simulations involving motion capture systems, their fielders have become more agile and responsive.

The individual players themselves have developed using technology, too. Professional cricketers use wearable devices and AI-powered training programmes that help them to hone their catching techniques and get the stumping right more often. And it is all of this that combines to make professional fielding better, and more like the catches that we see in the movies.

4.4: Conclusion

Top fielders not only have exceptional catching ability, but also a capacity to read the game as it unfolds. AI techniques are increasingly being applied to help improve these attributes. As one example, motion capture VR training environments have been developed for fielders that allow for personalised feedback on suboptimal reactions in terms of position and movement. This VR platform simulates real-world cricket matches in a trainable and immersive environment. There is also emerging work in predictive analytics with the application of AI to understand how player behaviours vary across different cricket competitions. In parallel with these developments, researchers have also considered the potential for 'smart' wearable devices (i.e., AI-powered wearables) that provide real-time feedback to fielders in terms of optimal strategies or play. Going forward, the proliferation of Guided Technique Series (GTS) AI apps will widen the scope of improvement opportunities.

CHAPTER FIVE

Revolutionizing Cricket: The Impact of AI on the Game

5.1: Predicting the Outcome of Cricket Matches

5.1.1: Introduction to AI in Sports Analytics

The integration of artificial intelligence (AI) into sports analytics marks a pivotal shift in how data is utilized to enhance performance, strategy, and fan engagement. AI's ability to process vast amounts of data and identify patterns that are imperceptible to the human eye has transformed many sports, with cricket being a prime beneficiary. In cricket, where strategy and statistics play crucial roles, AI's analytical prowess provides teams with a competitive edge by offering predictive insights that can significantly influence match outcomes.

5.1.2: Predictive Algorithms in Cricket

AI-driven predictive algorithms are at the forefront of cricket analytics. These algorithms analyse historical data, including player performances, pitch conditions, weather forecasts, and team compositions, to forecast the outcomes of matches with remarkable accuracy. Machine learning models, a subset of AI, are particularly adept at this task. They continuously learn and improve their predictions by processing new data and refining their models based on previous results.

One of the primary applications of predictive algorithms in cricket is match outcome prediction. By evaluating variables such as a team's batting and bowling strengths, the condition of the pitch, and historical performance data, AI can predict the likelihood of a team winning or losing. These predictions help coaches and players strategize more effectively, allowing them to make informed decisions about player selection, batting order, and field placements.

5.1.3: Case Studies and Success Stories

Several case studies highlight the success of AI in predicting cricket match outcomes. For instance, during the 2019 Cricket World Cup, AI models accurately predicted several match results, including upsets and close contests. These models considered a myriad of factors, such as individual player statistics, team dynamics, and external conditions, to deliver predictions that closely mirrored the actual outcomes.

Another notable example is the Indian Premier League (IPL), where franchises increasingly rely on AI analytics to guide their strategies. Teams like the Mumbai Indians and Chennai Super Kings have used AI to analyse player performances and opponent weaknesses, resulting in better match strategies and higher win rates.

5.1:4: AI in Real-Time Strategy

AI's role extends beyond pre-match predictions to real-time strategy adjustments. During a game, AI systems can process live data feeds, analysing every ball's trajectory, speed, and spin, along with players' positions and movements. This real-time analysis enables coaches and captains to make instantaneous decisions, such as field adjustments, bowling changes, and batting strategies.

For example, if a particular bowler is identified as being particularly effective against a specific type of batsman, AI can suggest deploying that bowler at crucial moments. Similarly, if a batsman is struggling against a particular delivery type, AI can recommend changes in the batting order to mitigate this weakness.

5.1.5: Conclusion

The integration of AI into cricket analytics has revolutionized how the game is played and strategized. Predictive algorithms provide teams with invaluable insights into match outcomes, enabling them to craft more effective strategies and make better-informed decisions. As AI technology continues to evolve, its impact on cricket is likely to grow, further enhancing the game's strategic depth and excitement.

In summary, the adoption of AI in predicting cricket match outcomes exemplifies the transformative power of technology in sports. By leveraging historical data and real-time analysis, AI not only helps teams win matches but also enriches the overall cricketing experience for players, coaches, and fans alike. The future of cricket, with AI as a key player, promises a more strategic, data-driven approach to the game, heralding a new era of innovation and excellence in the sport.

5.2: Enhancing Player Performance and Safety

5.2.1: Injury Prevention and Management

One of the most critical aspects of sports management is ensuring the health and safety of athletes. In cricket, where players face intense physical demands and risks of injuries, AI is becoming a game-changer. AI-powered systems are increasingly used to monitor players' physical conditions and predict potential injuries before they occur. By analysing data from wearable devices, such as heart rate monitors, GPS trackers, and motion sensors, AI can detect signs of fatigue, stress, and other risk factors that might lead to injuries.

For instance, a fast bowler's workload can be closely monitored to prevent overuse injuries. AI can analyse the number of deliveries bowled, the intensity of each delivery, and recovery times between spells. If the data indicates an increased risk of injury, the system can alert coaches to adjust the bowler's training or playing schedule. This proactive approach helps in maintaining player health and prolonging their careers.

5.2.2: Wearable Technology and AI

Wearable technology has revolutionized the way player performance and health are monitored. Devices such as smartwatches, fitness bands, and specialized sports equipment are equipped with sensors that collect real-time data on various physiological and biomechanical parameters. AI algorithms process this data to provide actionable insights.

For example, a batsman wearing a sensor-equipped vest can have their movements analysed in detail. AI can identify inefficiencies in their batting technique, such as improper weight distribution or suboptimal bat swing mechanics. By addressing these issues, players can improve their performance and reduce the risk of injury.

5.2.3: Optimizing Training Regimens

AI's ability to analyse vast amounts of data makes it invaluable for designing personalized training programs. Traditional training methods often rely on generalized routines that may not cater to individual players' specific needs. AI, however, can create customized regimens based on each player's strengths, weaknesses, and injury history.

For example, an AI system might analyse a player's performance data and determine that their batting against spin bowling is weaker than against fast bowling. The system can then recommend targeted drills and practice sessions to improve their skills against spinners. Similarly, for bowlers, AI can suggest modifications in their action to increase efficiency and reduce injury risk.

5.2.4: AI in Scoring and Performance Analysis

Scoring in cricket has traditionally been a manual process, prone to human error. AI-driven scoring systems automate this process, ensuring accuracy and providing deeper insights into player performances. These systems use computer vision and machine learning to track the ball, recognize player actions, and record every detail of the match.

Performance analysis, too, has been transformed by AI. Advanced algorithms can break down every aspect of a player's game, from batting and bowling techniques to fielding efficiency. Coaches and analysts can access comprehensive reports that highlight areas for improvement and suggest strategies to enhance performance. This level of detailed analysis was previously unattainable and allows for more precise and effective coaching.

5.2.6: Conclusion

The integration of AI into cricket has brought about significant advancements in player performance and safety. By leveraging wearable technology and sophisticated algorithms, AI helps prevent injuries, optimize training regimens, and provide accurate performance analyses. This technology not only enhances the individual capabilities of players but also contributes to the overall success and longevity of their careers.

Injury prevention through AI monitoring systems ensures that players can maintain their peak physical condition and avoid long-term damage. Personalized training programs tailored to each player's unique needs enable them to reach their full potential. Additionally, AI-driven scoring and performance analysis offer unprecedented levels of insight, allowing for more informed decision-making both on and off the field.

In essence, AI's role in enhancing player performance and safety represents a monumental shift in how cricket is played, coached, and managed. As AI technology continues to evolve, its applications in cricket will undoubtedly expand, leading to even greater improvements in player health, performance, and the overall quality of the game. This proactive and data-driven approach ensures that cricket remains a sport where skill and strategy are paramount, supported by cutting-edge technology that prioritizes the well-being of its players.

5.3: Transforming the Cricket Ecosystem

5.3.1: AI in Umpiring

Artificial Intelligence is revolutionizing umpiring in cricket, significantly enhancing the accuracy and fairness of decisions. Traditional umpiring, despite its reliance on human expertise, is susceptible to errors due to the fast-paced nature of the game. AI technologies, such as Hawk-Eye and Ultra Edge, have been integrated into the Decision Review System (DRS), providing umpires with precise tools to make better judgments.

Hawk-Eye technology tracks the ball's trajectory, offering a visual representation of its path, which is crucial for decisions on LBW (leg before wicket) and boundary calls. Ultra Edge, on the other hand, uses sound and video data to detect edges, ensuring correct decisions on caught behind dismissals. These AI-powered systems reduce the margin of error and increase the credibility of umpiring decisions, making the game fairer and more transparent.

5.3.2: Recruiting the Next Generation of Talent

AI's impact on recruiting talent is profound, transforming how cricket teams identify and nurture emerging players. Traditional scouting methods rely heavily on subjective judgments and limited data. AI, however, can analyse vast amounts of data from various sources, including domestic leagues, junior tournaments, and even school cricket matches, to identify potential stars.

Machine learning algorithms evaluate player performance metrics, such as batting averages, strike rates, bowling economy, and consistency, to predict future success. Additionally, AI can assess a player's adaptability, mental toughness, and potential for improvement by analysing historical performance trends. This data-driven approach enables teams to make more informed decisions when recruiting young talent, ensuring they invest in players with the highest potential for success.

For example, IPL teams have started using AI to scout talent from local and international leagues. AI systems analyse player statistics, playing styles, and even social media behaviour to gauge a player's marketability and potential impact on the team. This comprehensive analysis helps teams build stronger, more balanced squads, maximizing their chances of success.

5.3.3: Future Cricket Stadiums

Cricket stadiums are also set to evolve with the advent of AI, addressing the modern demands of the game and enhancing the spectator experience. One of the primary challenges in contemporary cricket is the increased power of bats, leading to more frequent sixes and boundaries. AI can aid in designing future stadiums that accommodate these changes while maintaining the competitive balance.

AI can simulate various design scenarios, optimizing stadium dimensions, boundary lengths, and seating arrangements to create the ideal environment for both players and spectators. These simulations consider factors such as player safety, spectator visibility, and environmental impact, ensuring that the stadiums of the future are both functional and sustainable.

Moreover, AI-driven crowd management systems can enhance the spectator experience by analysing foot traffic patterns, optimizing entry and exit points, and predicting areas of congestion. These systems improve safety and convenience, making cricket matches more enjoyable for fans.

5.3.4: Innovations in Bat Manufacturing

The manufacturing of cricket bats is another area where AI is making significant strides. Traditionally, bats are crafted based on general standards, with some customization for individual players. AI, however, allows for highly personalized bat manufacturing, optimizing wood distribution and bat weight according to each player's unique playing style.

AI systems analyse a player's batting technique, shot preferences, and physical attributes to recommend the ideal bat specifications. For example, a player who frequently plays aggressive shots may benefit from a heavier bat with a thicker edge, while a player who relies on timing and placement may prefer a lighter bat with a more even weight distribution.

This level of customization not only enhances player performance but also reduces the risk of injuries caused by using equipment that is not suited to their style. Bat manufacturers are increasingly adopting AI to create bespoke bats that cater to the specific needs of each player, offering them a competitive edge.

5.3.5: Conclusion

AI is fundamentally transforming the cricket ecosystem, from umpiring and talent recruitment to stadium design and equipment manufacturing. By enhancing the accuracy of umpiring decisions, AI ensures a fairer game. In talent recruitment, AI identifies promising players more effectively, allowing teams to build stronger squads. Future cricket stadiums, designed with AI simulations, will offer improved experiences for players and fans alike. Innovations in bat manufacturing, driven by AI, provide players with equipment tailored to their unique styles, optimizing performance and reducing injury risks.

As AI continues to advance, its applications in cricket will expand further, driving innovation and excellence in every aspect of the game. Embracing AI's potential ensures that cricket remains a dynamic, exciting sport, where technology and tradition work together to enhance the experience for players, coaches, and fans.

5.4: Conclusion: Embracing the AI Revolution in Cricket

Artificial Intelligence is no longer a futuristic concept but a present reality, transforming cricket in unprecedented ways. The integration of AI into various facets of the game signifies a monumental shift in how cricket is played, managed, and experienced. From enhancing player performance and safety to revolutionizing umpiring, recruiting, and infrastructure, AI is redefining cricket's landscape.

5.4.1: Summary of AI's Contributions

The contributions of AI to cricket are multi-faceted and profound. In match prediction, AI algorithms analyse vast datasets to forecast outcomes, providing teams with strategic insights that were previously unattainable. This predictive capability extends to in-game strategy adjustments, allowing teams to respond dynamically to evolving match situations. The predictive prowess of AI not only adds a layer of strategic depth but also brings a scientific approach to decision-making in cricket.

Injury prevention and player performance optimization are other significant areas where AI has made its mark. By leveraging wearable technology, AI monitors players' physical conditions in real-time, predicting potential injuries and suggesting pre-emptive measures. Customized training regimens tailored by AI ensure that each player can maximize their potential while minimizing the risk of injury. This data-driven approach to player management enhances longevity and overall performance, contributing to the sustained success of cricket teams.

AI has also revolutionized the accuracy and fairness of umpiring. Technologies like Hawk-Eye and Ultra Edge provide precise data that aids umpires in making more accurate decisions, reducing human error, and increasing the credibility of the game. This technological assistance ensures that matches are decided by skill and strategy rather than officiating errors, maintaining the sport's integrity.

Recruiting talent has never been more efficient, thanks to AI. By analysing comprehensive datasets, AI identifies potential stars early in their careers, allowing teams to invest in players with the highest potential for success. This methodical approach to talent scouting ensures that the next generation of cricket stars is identified and nurtured with precision.

The design of future cricket stadiums is another area poised for transformation through AI. By simulating various design scenarios, AI helps create stadiums that meet the modern demands of cricket while enhancing the spectator experience. From optimizing boundary lengths to managing crowd flow, AI ensures that new stadiums are functional, safe, and enjoyable for all.

Lastly, AI-driven innovations in bat manufacturing are providing players with equipment tailored to their unique styles. This customization not only enhances performance but also reduces the risk of injury, demonstrating AI's role in even the finer details of cricket.

5.4.2: Looking Ahead

The future of AI in cricket is bound to bring even more exciting advancements. As AI technology continues to evolve, its applications will become more sophisticated and integrated into every aspect of the game. Future developments might include AI-driven coaching assistants that provide real-time advice during matches, further enhancing strategic depth. Additionally, advancements in AI could lead to more immersive fan experiences, such as augmented reality (AR) and virtual reality (VR) integrations, bringing fans closer to the action than ever before.

AI's potential to analyse and simulate scenarios could also revolutionize cricket training. Virtual simulations powered by AI could allow players to practice against virtual opponents tailored to mimic the styles of real-world players, providing invaluable preparation for upcoming matches. Moreover, AI could play a critical role in cricket administration, optimizing scheduling, logistics, and even fan engagement strategies.

5.4.3: Embracing AI for a Better Game

The cricket community, from players and coaches to administrators and fans, must embrace AI's potential to ensure the sport's continued growth and evolution. While the integration of AI presents challenges, such as ensuring data security and maintaining the human element of the game, the benefits far outweigh the drawbacks. By adopting AI technologies, cricket can enhance fairness, performance, and enjoyment, ensuring that the sport remains competitive and captivating in the digital age.

In conclusion, AI's transformative impact on cricket is undeniable. From predicting match outcomes and preventing injuries to revolutionizing umpiring and personalizing equipment, AI is enhancing every aspect of the game. As we look to the future, the continued integration of AI promises to bring even greater innovations, driving cricket towards a new era of excellence and excitement. Embracing AI not only ensures the sport's relevance in the modern world but also enriches the cricketing experience for players and fans alike. The AI revolution in cricket is just beginning, and its potential to elevate the game to new heights is limitless.

PART-THREE

FOOTBALL:

Chapter 6: Scoring Goals: AI-Assisted Training for Strikers

Chapter 7: Goalkeeping Mastery: AI for the Last Line of Defence

CHAPTER SIX

Scoring Goals: AI-Assisted Training for Strikers

6.1: Shot Accuracy and Power

Let's use scoring a goal as an example from football. Scoring is the most obvious signature of any successful striker, and bringing this skill to perfection takes going beyond natural talent and regular training to aim for sheer logic. By courtesy of AI, the means of training isn't left at simple drills on the field. The modern striker can have even more edge in learning to score.

AI tools can do much more than just this in terms of providing a level of understanding, with personalised analyses and feedback that was unimaginable without modern training methods. Accuracy also emerges as a crucial factor in the conceptual performance analysis of strikers. The advent of AI-powered video analysis systems has allowed for highly detailed studies of player behaviour by recording footage of strikers' shooting technique in high-definition while training and playing. This technology can then be employed to enhance the skill level of a striker. The videos can be processed with machine-learning algorithms that look for unintended deviations between perfect form and reality. These collected data can then be analysed to point out where the striker's body posture, positioning of their feet or their final follow-through deviated off the expected pattern.

For example, the ball's flight path to the goal can be studied by AI moment by moment from the moment it is struck by the striker's foot to the moment it strikes the net. By comparing the flight path of goals with thousands of shots that have resulted in successes, AI can provide specific information about angle and force to score at a designated point. In this way, players can tweak their technique as the shot develops. They can adjust their stance, for example, or adopt a different striking action.

Furthermore, sensors embedded in wearable technology can boost shot power. Such devices measure certain biomechanical variables like leg speed, angle of impingement and force exerted by the foot, with AI algorithms interpreting the data to explain how a striker can hit harder without spoiling their accuracy. If the analysis of the sensor data reveals that a player's leg speed, for instance, is insufficient to send a shot into the top corner of the net, exercises can be targeted to boost muscle strength and flexibility.

AI is also compatible with technical adjustments made by strikers on the pitch. Match data may reveal the striker's shooting patterns – high volume in the centre, or recurrent weakness near the sideline – along with tendencies when they're under pressure, such as shooting immediately, using their favoured foot or a particular part of the field. AI analysis can yield targeted recommendations, such as expanding their range of shooting positions, or increasing their situational awareness under extreme duress. If a striker frequently produces weak shots at the left side of the penalty area, AI might employ visualisation and drills to enhance match outcomes in that part of the field.

AI-enhanced virtual reality (VR) training further expands the striker's capacity to work on accuracy and power at shooting: VR platforms create realistic match scenarios in which the AI-controlled players display human-like reactions to shots – for instance, dodging, blocking lines of sight, moving closer or further according to the situation, etc. VR reproduces live-match conditions for the striker and allows him or her to work on the nuances of shooting in different conditions and against various types of defences. The immersive nature of VR training equips the striker's body to acquire 'muscle memory' in the classroom. That same muscle memory is then sourced subconsciously during Matchplay under heavy pressure.

6.2: Positioning and Movement Analysis

Sure, a striker should be a good technician – but if they lack smart positioning and movement, then they won't create the space for scoring goals. AI is changing how strikers think about positioning and movement, offering insights into the strategy of the game that were once unattainable.

Striker positioning patterns are being analysed by AI systems that process billions of match data points to determine optimal positions on the field. According to the player tracking systems, the AI can analyse patterns from goals that were previously deemed unlikely. If we contextualise certain aspects of the match – say, the phase of the match, the location of the cut, the position of the goalkeeper relative to the attacker – or match state – sub context 43 – we can see that the player in question was in exceptionally good position to score a goal. With a machine capable of statistical modelling and learning, a striker's positioning can easily be adjusted in-game to be in the right spot at the right time.

Movement analysis is another important application where AI plays an important role. Tracking systems employ AI to study a striker's movements during a match, and provide detailed feedback on their speed, agility and mobility. Machines learn to recognise certain patterns in a striker's relative movement with respect to teammates and opponents, indicating areas where they need to be more agile and responsive.

In one example, if the data suggests that a striker is frequently offside or that he needs to be in a better position to open up space, AI can prescribe specific drills to help him with his spatial awareness and movement timing. The striker can practise these drills in a controlled environment, and then the AI can provide feedback on how to make further incremental adjustments. After a period of working with the technology, these adjustments will result in better movement, the striker can start to get away from defenders more frequently and be in a better position to make goalscoring opportunities.

And training intelligence can be engineered using AI to adapt to a striker's changing training needs on a tennis court or a rugby pitch. Such programs can monitor the striker's performance data as it evolves, mapping it against opponent statistics, and continuously adjust training location, duration and intensity according to the striker's latest needs.

At the same time, tactical analysis from AI allows the striker to situate his role within the overall context of the team's offensive strategy – for example, studying team-based positional organisation, playing style and formation will enable the striker to operate more strategically as part of the team's goal-scoring efforts. These are just some of the ways in which athletes will soon benefit from competent assistance from AI in the near term, before seamlessly moving from assistive to collaborative AI.

6.3 :Real-World Applications and Case Studies

There have already been success stories of teams and players who have seen the benefits of it on the pitch. Manchester City, for example, have harnessed AI to break down their match footage to improve the performance of their strikers, according to The New York Times. Liverpool is also used to using AI systems to track performance metrics to improve training regimes – and their attacking stars are all the better for it. As a result of this hybridised training, the players are now scoring more goals.

Players too are benefiting from AI-enhanced training methods. Cristiano Ronaldo and Lionel Messi are among those who have fine-tuned their shooting, sharpened their spacing and positioning on the field, and discovered secret techniques that have transformed them into some of the greatest scorers of all time. The figures speak for themselves.

6.4: Conclusion

AI-assisted training has been central to the development of modern footballers, introducing new ways of enhancing a striker's shooting and movement, in particular. Based on advanced video analysis and goal-by-goal data, companies are now creating personalised variabilities that supplement the shot accuracy, power, movement and positioning of the striker. All this is coupled with wearable technology and virtual reality training. AI in football is just getting started, even if it's already being used on the sidelines, in training, in scouting reports and even in designing boot soles. It will provide increasingly sophisticated tools to those who aim to become the Leonidas of the future. In the coming years, football as a sport will grow increasingly rich and dense from a strategic angle, thanks to AI's contributions.

CHAPTER SEVEN

Goalkeeping Mastery: AI for the Last Line of Defence

7.1: Reaction Time and Save Techniques

Football goalkeeping is a very demanding position that requires excellent reflexes, extreme mobility and, above all, a good decision-making process. The room for error is small, and having fast reactions can make the difference between preventing a goal or allowing one in. AI can leverage machine learning to improve reaction times and save techniques.

Thanks to AI systems with advanced motion capture and analysis, goalkeepers' reflexes and save techniques will improve Additionally, data points are captured by high-speed cameras or solutions with sensors that are placed both on the ball and the goalkeeper's hands. Whether it's saving headers or close-range shots, the AI takes into account every detail on the field. Each data point is used by AI algorithms to compare and form patterns between the goalkeeper's respondent reactions to different kicks and saves on goal. By tracking the ball's trajectory alongside the goalkeeper's hand movements, AI can gauge whether an improvement of the goalkeeper's reaction time can be enhanced with a different stance or positioning.

For example, goalkeepers can wear sensors in their fingertips in the form of smart gloves so that they can get feedback on hand and finger position in real time and make immediate adjustments to their technique to improve their save percentages.

Goalkeepers can practise their reflexes and saving techniques in immersive VR training environments It produces VR training environments where goalkeepers can practise their reflexes and saving techniques in a realistic and immersive fashion, including against fast-moving shots, deflections, one-on-one scenarios and other plausibly challenging situations. In these environments, the AI produces shots that adapt in terms of complexity and frequency (both in total number of shots over time and with respect to the type of actual and perceived threat), building up the difficulty of the task as the goalkeeper learns and improves.

AI is increasingly important for assessing and optimising a goalkeeper's diving technique: by considering the trajectory of the ball and the position of the goal from a broad perspective (side-on), AI can model the right-angled triangular relationship between all three elements and identify what biomechanical adjustments will allow for the maximum coverage of the space covered by the goal (which is effectively the hypotenuse of the triangle). For example, if the trajectory shows the ball falling short of the goalie, analysis of the goalie's dive from above will allow for assessments of things such as body angle, leg extension and arm reach. A deeper dive requires adaptations to core strength and flexibility.

7.2: Predictive Positioning and Opponent Analysis

They can also improve reaction time and save techniques. It is well-known that being prepared to act on an event is largely determined by the way one is primed to expect that event. Information that is unavailable, and cannot be provided to the decision-maker, is foreknowledge of an event that they were not in a position to predict or make use of in their decision-making. This is essentially the difference between Positive Predictive Value in a statistical hypothesis test, and the rarely discussed negative predictive value (that rare events won't happen). The probability of the correct outcome of a medical diagnostic is an example of Positive Predictive Value. The probability that a healthy patient will not develop a disease is a negative predictive value – information that simply isn't relevant to the care of a healthy patient. ATP is unavailable information that, if possessed, could affect how we decide in a situation. By utilizing AI technology, a goalkeeper can improve their predictive positioning and opponent-analysis skills, in addition to any impact it may have on reaction times and save techniques.

Such a system might evaluate, based on incredible range and number of inputs, the odds that the goalkeeper will be presented with a specific kind of shot at a certain location, based on hundreds of previous match data points that have been mined for information about the tendencies and patterns of opposing players in situations resembling the one the goalkeeper presently faces: are they left-footed or right; do they shoot to the keeper's left or right; do they shoot from left to right and vice-versa; is their coach an ex-goalkeeper who has beaten them all his life? With a surprisingly simple machine-learning algorithm, the goalie could be coached to predict with high probability where a shot from the opposing side is going to come from. Here is an example, a long one, but it illustrates the underlying idea at work to perfection: If we now superimpose on this autonomous sensory-motor activity the essential content of the goal-keeper's job we get … Bridging cognitive normativity, which relates to true-or-false assertions and to reasons for belief, with a new kind of normativity, which relates to the distinctively motivating force of reasons for action, might seem impossible; after all, beliefs involve contents and no actions do.

An AI algorithm produces a heat map of the goal, which illustrates the most targeted spots for a certain player or team. In turn, this can let a keeper know where to go more often during a game, to maximise his chances of catching a ball. Say an opponent is known for always shooting a corner spot, in this case, the top left, the keeper's positioning could be a few centimetres closer to that area, and that could make the difference to keep a shot from slipping past them.

In addition, goalkeepers can look back at game footage, using AI to help them observe and analyse their positioning and movements relative to play scenarios. For example, AI might highlight moments when the goalkeeper was slow getting off their line or was caught out of position. Onto the habituation: the AI can detect patterns from a goalkeeper's movement data and provide feedback about the logic behind their decisions. In turn, this AI feedback can help the goalkeeper habituate a more adaptable set of goals toward anticipating play; for instance, they might want to minimise the number of times they're slow getting off their line.

Predictive analytics could also come into play here. Corner kicks and free-kicks, for example, are all set-piece situations where the ball is kicked at a specific distance and angle, and defenders move to find places to block passes, challenges the ball or just keep their opposing team away from the goal area. Some AI systems can analyse how a particular team executes these plays and the patterns they follow including where on the field they place the ball, how many players they move forward to block a pass to the striking player, potential targeting zones of the strikers, and the most common type of set-up by the opposing team in defence such as double and triple marking. Goalkeepers can use study the patterns revealed by AI to improve their positioning and responses to set pieces.

Traditional tactical analysis tools – where coaches review a team's performance after a game – can be augmented by tactical tools that provide real-time feedback during matches. Wearable devices fitted to, for example, a goalkeeper could monitor their positioning and movement, and transmit the data to one or more AI systems that could analyse the information and provide instant advice on how to adjust their positioning. If a goalkeeper is far too often too far off their line, or misjudging the angle of an oncoming attacker, the AI could provide details that suggest adjustments in play that would improve the goalkeeper's performance.

7.3: Real-World Applications and Case Studies

Many of the world's top football clubs and national teams have started using AI in goalkeeping training, as have many of their individual keepers. FC Bayern Munich and Real Madrid both use AI in their training tools, in which they analyse film from matches and from training sessions and compose individual training programmes around their goalies.

Certainly, most individual goalkeepers like Manuel Neuer in Germany and Alisson Becker in Brazil, have also benefitted from the application of AI technologies to improve their reactions within the last few years, which has not only enhanced their save techniques but ultimately their positioning. They've shown how good goalkeeping work can be enhanced using AI to improve individual and team performance.

7.4: Conclusion

Wearing motion capture systems or ML-augmented wearables, goalkeepers can train their reaction times, refine save techniques, learn more predictive positioning, build a memory of opponents, and receive personalised feedback and targeted training. AI in goalkeeping may soon extend to new arsenal of smarter tools for goalkeepers, thanks to advances in motion-capture systems, virtual reality training environments and predictive analytics. Some advanced algorithms are already capable of predicting goalkeepers' and attackers' movements through their bodies' interactions with the ball and team plays. Partnering with AI in their training ultimately increases the strategic depth and competitiveness of football teams. This can only mean that the future of goalkeeping will be informed by precision and data insights.

PART-FOUR

TRACK AND FIELD:

Chapter 8: Marathon Running: Endurance and Strategy with AI

8.1 Training regimes and endurance building.

8.2 Race strategy and pacing.

8.3 Real-World applications & Case Studies

8.4 Conclusion

Chapter 9: AI Techniques for 100-Meter Dash: Speed and Power

9.1 Sprint mechanics and starting block techniques.

9.2 Enhancing acceleration and top speed.

9.3 Real-World Applications & Case studies

9.4 Conclusion

Chapter 10: Short-Distance Running: Combining Speed and Strategy

10.1 Interval training and speed drills.

10.2 Race tactics and mental preparation.

10.3 Real-World Applications & Case Studies

10.4 Conclusion

CHAPTER EIGHT

Marathon Running: Endurance and Strategy with AI

8.1: Training Regimes and Endurance Building

Marathon running is an exceptionally challenging and demanding athletic event, calling for more than just physical conditioning and reserved energy. Whether tackled competitively or leisurely, it's imperative for any aspiring marathon runner to develop a mental resilience against faltering and fatigue while also properly fuelling the body for stamina and endurance. Training regimens for marathon runners typically entail pre-tuning the biology with regularly scheduled long-distance runs, interval training, and a sustainable supplementation of carbohydrates and proteins in the diet itself. However, a game-changer has arrived— Artificial Intelligence (AI)—which has greatly enhanced the way one prepares to undertake this formidable challenge.

An AI-commanded training regime design propels athletes to fitness rooted in each individual runner's needs, adapting along the way. Training begins with a baseline evaluation of critical parameters such as VO2max (the maximum volume of oxygen a person can consume per unit of time, typically measured during exercise to gauge a person's cardiovascular fitness), lactate threshold (the maximum intensity load during running or cycling before the onset of fatigue) and running economy (a measure of how efficiently the cardiovascular and neuromuscular systems work while running). Thanks to wearable devices outfitted with cutting-edge sensors, data collectors record heart rates, stride lengths, cadences and other biomechanical variables in real time during training sessions. This information feeds into AI algorithms to formulate a high-definition fitness profile.

Using this profile, AI systems will then recommend personalised training programmes based on the best ratio between training volume (total distance) and training intensity (relative speed and effort level). For example, if a given runner's data recommends an increase in aerobic capacity, the AI can recommend endurance runs at low speeds. If the runner's data reflects a lower lactate threshold, the AI can recommend high-intensity interval training (HIIT) sessions.

Acting as the coach, AI can also monitor how the runner is progressing and adjust in real time. It can draw on the athlete's performance data by continuously processing historical information. If it sees the athlete's heart rate is consistently high during workouts, it can reduce the intensity: if the heart rate is creeping up during a long run, suggesting the risk of overtraining, the system could suggest running at an easier pace or adding days of rest. Rather than simply having performance feedback, the athlete works in partnership with the machine to minimise the risks of injury and maximise performance over the long term.

In addition, thousands of these AI carers are used to offer real-time feedback and motivation to people training for a marathon. The virtual training coach can lead runners through their workouts, giving tips about form, pacing and breathing. It can also mimic the feel of race day to help prepare runners for the challenge.

8.2: Race Strategy and Pacing

This sentimental touch, while common for both athletes and machines, disguises the deeper ways in which AI has become essential to the marathon. Beyond training and nutrition, sophisticated race strategies are needed to best during the long-distance event. Your machine-coach helps with these strategies, too, by calculating optimal speeds to hit target times, considering data ranging from the start-flag time to your resting heart rate and average stride length. Your assistant intuitively knows when to slow you down and when to speed you up, maximising your potential in every mile and minimising fatigue with laser-honed precision.

One of the most important elements in a race strategy is pacing. For each participant, a complex pacing strategy is informed by hours of data analysis on past races, current fitness, and environmental context, such as course elevation and weather. If the course has a long, gradual uphill, AI could determine that the pace in the first part of the race should be slower than planned so that an increase in the pace (wringing out faster times downhill and on flats) can result in finishing the course more quickly than expected.

AI-driven simulators can allow runners to practise their pacing in a safe setting beforehand More precisely, virtual race simulators can re-create the complete conditions of an upcoming marathon, including the course profile and the prevailing weather conditions. With this type of training, runners can fine-tune their pacing strategy to match elite runners and be well-prepared for race day.

The second aspect is energy management, which allows AI to help runners optimise their energy expenditure through personalised fuelling and hydration strategies. Based on the runner's underlying metabolism and expected race-day conditions, the AI will recommend precise times throughout the marathon to sip carbohydrate and hydrate the body, keeping the runner primed for optimal performance. This helps the runner avoid 'hitting the wall', in which energy levels drown and the legs begins to feel heavy, leading to a deterioration in pace.

Providing continuous feedback during a race AI-powered analytics can also adjust strategy on-the-fly, when the marathon is running. Data from wearable tech, tracking the runner's body – pace, position, breathing, sweat, heart rate and so on – provides continuous feedback on their performance and physiology, at every moment of the marathon. If the runner deviates from the optimal pace, or if their body signals distress, the AI might advise them to lower their pace, temporarily, and recover their reserves before returning to the target pace.

Beyond that, an AI runner can analyse the competition and respond to variables based on what other runners are doing. Take data on other athletes' past race-distance performance, and an AI can discern well in advance of a run when the optimal moment might arrive to accelerate pace – to overtake a rival who has depleted a sprint frequently, for example – or when it might be better to feign fatigue and lull others into making a move, waiting for the final sprint to reload and make a clean win. So we have competition, a second dynamic of strategy beyond the direct problem-solving dynamic between an AI and its environment.

8.3: Real-World Applications and Success Stories

The impact of AI on marathon training and strategy has been significant. Many top marathoners and elite professional running teams have adopted AI training to help improve performance. In fact, the Nike Breaking2 Project, where runners attempted to break the two-hour marathon barrier, leveraged massive data sets to inform training regimens, pacing strategies and even led to the creation of race-shoe optimisation. The project fell short of breaking the two-hour mark in an official marathon, but nonetheless demonstrated AI's ability to push the limits of human performance.

But amateurs have also been the beneficiaries of AI. Nearly all running apps and wearable devices now incorporate certain AI functionality, using algorithms that create personalised training plans and instant and occasional coaching. Advanced training techniques that were once the preserve of specialised applications with PhDs are now widely available – and they do help athletes of all stripes get faster and stay injury-free often. And they also make the experience of running that much more pleasurable.

8.4: Conclusion

AI is primarily affecting training and strategy in marathon running. It provides runners with personalised (i.e. different for each runner) and adaptive (i.e. changing over time depending upon data about the runner's response) tools to develop stronger endurance and achieve greater performance during races. More precisely, to provide runners with customised training programmes, AI analyses runners' fitness data, thereby allowing the computer to propose the most effective training regime. This training regime is specifically designed to maximise physical preparation for endurance and racing while at the same time minimising the risk of injuries. Furthermore, AI is also affecting marathon running from a strategic point of view. More precisely, as a pacing and race strategy tool, AI provides runners with specifications regarding how they should pace their race to achieve greater performance. This might include for example the runner's desired pace over each kilometre of the race, as well as specific instructions about the timing of refuelling and rehydrating over the course of the race. It is expected that AI technology will continue to evolve until it become capable of improving all aspects related to marathon running goodness – in other words, how to develop their endurance and how to organise the race to maximise the number of runners' fun while maintaining the prestige of the competition. The integration of AI is not only contributing to greater personal and athletic performance, to the growth of sophisticated technology, and to the expansion of sport, but also to making all of this more accessible to more runners. This in turn is increasing the number of individuals who can achieve runners' goals and help push human beings' physical and psychological boundaries.

CHAPTER NINE

AI Techniques for 100-Meter Dash: Speed and Power

9.1: Sprint Mechanics and Starting Block Techniques

The 100-metre dash is a race of rhythm, power and explosive speed measured in hundredths of a second. An athlete's sprinting mechanics and starting strategy must be mastered and perfected if they are to cross the finish line first. Now, artificial intelligence (AI) can help athletes train by analysing their running techniques, helping them anticipate one another and optimise their starts to eke out fractions of a second – what it takes to become an Olympic champion.

AI-powered analytics tools can also help with the biomechanics of sprinting. High-speed cameras and motion sensors capture detailed data on a sprinter's posture, angles of limbs and joints, and the force each step puts into the ground. Algorithms across the pipeline feed this data into AI models that hunt for inefficiencies and unevenness that a coach's eye might miss. AI, for example, could study the angle at which a sprinter's upper body leaves the blocks as she rocks back, optimising her exit while minimising the vertical motion that leads to wasted energy.

The starting block phase is one of the most crucial for athletes competing in the 100-metre dash. A runner needs to be ready to produce their best performance from the very beginning. In this case, AI can be used to analyse the starting technique of a sprinter, including the position of their body and the initial push-off from the starting blocks. This way, an AI application can help you see which part of the body needs to be positioned more powerfully and where the push-off can improve, based on the distribution of forces, the timing between different parts of your body, and more. For example, if the force generated in your leg muscles isn't effective while you're pushing off the starting blocks, then AI may suggest about certain specific strength training exercises to improve your running performance.

Furthermore, in the case of personalised training, AI could provide continuous feedback in real time. Sensors can be used to measure skill execution on a sprinter, and human-sounding applications driven by AI can then immediately analyse captured data and suggest some tweaks. In this way, athletes can adjust tweaks on the fly to improve their form and technique, making for more effective training and faster learning curve.

9.2: Enhancing Acceleration and Top Speed

Once through the blocks, a sprinter must accelerate to maximum speed and then keep that speed through to the finish line. AI helps to maximise both the process of acceleration and maximum speed, which are delivered to the athlete as tools they use to do their job.

Acceleration in the 100-metre dash is a delicate mixture of strength, technique and timing. AI can parse the acceleration phase, identifying the critical points in time when an athlete should become less forceful and more efficient. When we break down the acceleration phase into smaller increments, we can pinpoint the specific improvements needed at each step of the progression. It might tell an athlete that their hips aren't reaching full extension as optimal on the first one or two steps, which results in a lower power output. With specific drills and strength work, an athlete can address this issue.

The top speed phase is equally important. During this section of a race, the sprinter is trying to maintain their maximum velocity, which is very important. AI driven tools can assist sprinters to fine-tune so that they can maintain their speed during the last part of their race. By analysing a sprinters mechanics, the AI can measure stride length and frequency through flow-sensing technology. The AI predicts the inefficiencies that might slow a sprinter down, like an early dip in stride frequency. For example, it might offer tips on how a sprinter can maintain stride frequency into the finish line, such as increasing muscle stability or improving the arm swing to make the legs turnover faster.

Likewise, it could help sprinters best utilise their physiological attributes by charting a course through the race that builds on their natural strengths and takes advantage of their opponent's sensed weaknesses. Thus, AI could examine an athlete's previous performances, along with his or her physiological data, to design a personalised training programme aimed optimising aspects of that athlete's performance. If a sprinter's weakness was a tendency to fade from top speed, for example, an AI trainer might recommend a combination of strength, plyometrics and speed endurance training sessions.

The training feedback is AI-powered, too, though not in a purely impersonal way. You can confront race scenarios in training and prepare for races by running in virtual environments of different sizes, with different visibility conditions that affect how clearly – or not – athletes can see other runners in the race, and so on. It's more intuitive, training this way and allows the sprinters to adapt more effectively when they compete in smaller or larger races or with different visibility conditions.

9.3: Real-World Applications and Success Stories

Soon, the technology that underlies Future Sprint has become mainstream. The world's best runners and coaches are adopting AI to shape runners' technique and boost performance. Usain Bolt, arguably the greatest sprinter of all time, underwent advanced biomechanical analysis to fine-tune his running technique and reach peak explosive power.

In addition, sports technology firms such as Coach's Eye and Dartfish use machine learning to sift through big data to deliver visual-feedback video reviews to athletes. This enables them to view side-by-side comparison of pushing technical models and measure efficiencies to find areas for enhancement. For example, sprinters can review over-the-shoulder views of their starts to identify imperfections.

And even amateur sprinters and their trainers have access to some AI-powered services: apps for sprinting that offer real-time feedback, personalised training plans and even automated training routines are also on offer, all of which democratise advanced sprint training methods.

9.4: Conclusion

The introduction of AI has brought about significant advancements in training and performance-enhancement of sprinters, particularly those competing in the 100-metre dash, the premier event of a sporting meeting. AI's detailed biomechanical analysis and real-time feedback of sprinters' performance helps them perfect their sprint mechanics and optimises their starting block technique to enhance anticipatory capability. Furthermore, AI provides athletes with improved training programmes to achieve maximal acceleration and top-speed phases to ensure sprinters reach their optimal running and jumping potential. In the years to come, the applications of AI in sprinting training will create new and even more sophisticated training tools to help the next generation of elite sprinters enhance their sprint performance. Advanced technologies like AI will have a meaningful impact on all aspects of sprinting and its performance, offering training options and opportunities for athletes at all levels, and allowing them to reach new limits and improve their potential.

CHAPTER TEN

Short-Distance Running: Combining Speed and Strategy

Short distance running, which typically includes races ranging from 100 meters to 400 meters, is a blend of explosive speed, refined technique, and strategic thinking. To excel in these events, athletes must focus on developing both their physical capabilities and their mental strategies. The integration of interval training, speed drills, race tactics, and mental preparation forms the backbone of a comprehensive training regimen for short-distance runners.

10.1: Interval Training and Speed Drills

Interval training is a cornerstone of short distance running training programs. This method involves alternating periods of high-intensity sprints with low-intensity recovery periods. The primary goal of interval training is to enhance both aerobic and anaerobic capacity, allowing athletes to sustain high speeds over the entire race distance.

AI-driven interval training programs are particularly effective because they can tailor workouts to the specific needs of the athlete. Wearable technology equipped with advanced sensors can track an athlete's performance in real-time, including metrics such as heart rate, pace, and lactate threshold. AI algorithms analyse this data to design personalized interval sessions that optimize the balance between intensity and recovery.

For instance, a typical AI-designed interval workout for a 200-meter sprinter might include repeated sprints of 100 meters at maximum effort, followed by 30 seconds of rest, repeated multiple times. The AI can adjust the duration and intensity of these intervals based on the runner's progress, ensuring continuous improvement and adaptation.

Speed drills are another critical component of short distance running training. These drills focus on improving various aspects of sprinting technique, such as stride length, frequency, and running form. AI can enhance these drills by providing real-time feedback on an athlete's biomechanics. High-speed cameras and motion sensors capture detailed data on the runner's movements, which is then analysed to identify inefficiencies or technical flaws.

For example, AI might detect that a sprinter's foot placement is suboptimal, causing unnecessary drag and reducing speed. The system can suggest specific drills to correct this issue, such as high-knee runs, butt kicks, or A-skips. By continuously refining technique through targeted speed drills, athletes can improve their overall efficiency and speed.

10.2: Race Tactics and Mental Preparation

While physical training is crucial, short distance running also demands strategic thinking and mental toughness. Race tactics involve planning and executing a strategy that maximizes performance while accounting for the strengths and weaknesses of both the athlete and their competitors.

AI can play a significant role in developing and refining race tactics. By analysing data from previous races, AI can identify patterns and trends that inform strategic decisions. For instance, AI might analyse split times to determine the optimal pacing strategy for a 400-meter race. If data shows that the athlete consistently slows down in the final 100 meters, the AI might suggest a more conservative pace in the first 200 meters to conserve energy for a stronger finish.

Additionally, AI can simulate various race scenarios, allowing athletes to practice their tactics in a controlled environment. Virtual reality (VR) training tools can create realistic race simulations where runners can experience different pacing strategies, starting techniques, and race conditions. These simulations help athletes develop a more intuitive understanding of race dynamics and improve their decision-making skills during actual competitions.

Mental preparation is equally vital for short-distance runners. The high-stakes nature of these races means that even a minor lapse in focus or confidence can significantly impact performance. AI-driven mental training programs offer tools to enhance psychological resilience and focus.

One effective method is the use of biofeedback technology, which monitors physiological responses such as heart rate variability and galvanic skin response. AI algorithms analyse this data to assess the athlete's stress levels and emotional state. Based on this analysis, the system can provide personalized relaxation techniques, such as breathing exercises or visualization practices, to help the athlete maintain composure and focus.

Visualization is a particularly powerful tool in mental preparation. AI can create detailed visualizations of the race, allowing athletes to mentally rehearse every aspect of their performance. By vividly imagining the start, the acceleration phase, the sprint, and the finish, athletes can build confidence and reduce pre-race anxiety. This mental rehearsal helps create a sense of familiarity and preparedness, making it easier to execute the race plan under pressure.

10.3: Real-World Applications and Success Stories

The integration of AI in short-distance running has been embraced by elite athletes and coaches worldwide. Notable sprinters, such as Usain Bolt and Allyson Felix, have utilized AI-driven tools to enhance their training and performance. These athletes have benefited from personalized interval training programs, real-time biomechanical feedback, and advanced race simulations.

For example, Usain Bolt's training regimen included the use of high-speed cameras and motion analysis to refine his sprinting technique. By leveraging AI technology, Bolt was able to identify and correct inefficiencies in his form, contributing to his record-breaking performances.

Amateur runners also benefit from AI-driven training tools. Many fitness apps and wearable devices now incorporate AI features that provide personalized training plans, technique analysis, and mental preparation exercises. These tools make advanced training techniques accessible to a broader audience, helping everyday runners improve their performance and enjoy a more fulfilling running experience.

10.4: Conclusion

Short distance running requires a holistic approach that combines physical training with strategic planning and mental preparation. AI-driven interval training and speed drills help athletes enhance their speed and efficiency by providing personalized, data-driven insights and real-time feedback. AI also plays a crucial role in developing race tactics and mental resilience, enabling athletes to perform at their best under pressure. As AI technology continues to evolve, its applications in short-distance running will expand, offering even more sophisticated tools for athletes to excel. The integration of AI not only improves individual performance but also contributes to the overall advancement of the sport, enabling runners of all levels to achieve their full potential.

RUGBY:

CHAPTER ELEVEN

AI in Rugby: Tactics and Physical Conditioning

Rugby is a contact, high-peaks and troughs sport and requires skill, strategy, physical conditioning and more than just that, teamwork. AI with its emergence and the application within rugby whether that be in-game strategy, play analysis and preparation, or physical conditioning is changing the way we prepare, train and compete at every level.

11.1: Game Strategy and Play Analysis

Rugby is a masterclass in tactics: knowing the enemy's techniques and making the most of the team's plays can leave them sniffing your heels rather than dashing ahead. So, it's no surprise that AI is being used to is proving revolutionary, uncovering insights that would otherwise have been impossible to obtain.

By analysing data from previous matches, such as runs made by players, trajectories of passes, tackle success rates right up to micro-trends in set pieces such as scrums and lineouts, sophisticated machine learning can identify trends and patterns that can provide insights for tactical strategies. For a given team, their historical statistics enable applications of AI to identify opponent's most favoured attacking routes, weaknesses in their defence, key players driving play and so on.

To rugby, one of the game's biggest benefits from AI is in-game analysis: wearable GPS devices and shirts with embedded sensors that track both the movements and physiological metrics of players that are relayed to the side and coaches can immediately make tactical adjustments based off real-time AI-driven discoveries. For example, if the AI determines that the opposition is consistently using a particular wing play, the coaches and trainers might be moved to respond (by pushing up defensive bodies, or substituting someone more capable on defence, etc) too.

Not only that – AI tools can go further, by simulating a range of situations, giving teams the chance to experiment with tactics. VR simulations of match situations help players to experience scenarios and develop responses without having to expend energy during physical practise. By doing so, players can anticipate what an opponent is going to do, make quicker decisions under pressure and generally improve their game intelligence.

And post-match, AI-analysis provides a breakdown of the game in terms of team and individual performances, allowing the coach to review individual moments in the game to gauge the effectiveness of the strategy, identify and rectify mistakes, and improve the team's next performance. Indeed, with this lossless data feedback, a more iterative process or constant gauge can be achieved, where performance will become more strategic and informed.

11.2: Strength and Conditioning for Optimal Performance

As a brutal contact sport, rugby demands that players present a peculiar combination of strength, speed, endurance and agility. This requires players to be in top shape for every game. To achieve this, players undergo a personalised training plan devised by the coach, culminating in a rigorous off-season regime of intensive fitness training. Strength and conditioning programmes for sportsmen are undergoing a rapid evolution due to the influence of AI, which is now helping to provide personalised training plans, monitor performance and reduce injury risk.

AI-supported strength and conditioning programmes begin by profiling each player's physiological characteristics. Data from wearables and smart gym equipment is collected to determine current levels and weaknesses across key biomarkers such as maximal muscle strength, power output, flexibility, and aerobic fitness. The data can then be analysed by AI to determine optimal training areas to address, and plan training content based on overall needs and objectives. For a player who needs to improve their sprint speed, the AI might suggest a combination of plyometric exercise, resistance exercise, and interval running.

The ability to track players' progress in real time and adjust training loads accordingly is a key advantage of AI in conditioning. The AI tracks important training metrics in real time, such as heart rate, recovery times and workload, to help players train at the right intensity. The system can also sense if a player is getting worn down or is in danger of certain overuse injuries. It can then adjust a player's training programme, such as adding more rest days or lowering the intensity of the workouts.

Rugby injuries are an unfortunate big deal, not only in terms of health, but conditioning or training to decrease injury or pre-injury are lackadaisically inadequate in training regimens. AI holds natural applications in injury prevention. With the assistance of biomechanical data, AI can create predictive analytics by detecting movement patterns that could lead to injury. For example, if the AI perceives an injury risk based on an action, such as an improper landing mechanics in a jump (improper mechanics could cause a knee injury), it can direct an exercise and drill that the player needs to prevent or fix the issue.

There are also gains through AI with respect to recovery. Post-match and post-training recovery regimes are vital for players returning to full readiness for the next game or training session, and AI systems can generate personalised recovery plans based on activity intensity, the accumulated physiological data and the rate at which each player is recovering. These plans could provide recommendations, for example on hydration and nutrition, sleep, or specific recovery exercises to assist return to full performance as quickly as possible.

11.3: Real-World Applications and Success Stories

And this isn't all future-speak: it's already in use by the world's best teams and backed by the highest offices within today's rugby. Numbers don't lie. Professional teams in the English Premiership and the international Super Rugby competition are using AI for an edge.

A case in point, the New Zealand All Blacks rugby team, one of the most successful sports teams in history, some might argue, the best, has used AI to help them prepare for their opponents, basically learning from competitor video footage and adjusting so that everyone paid attention to the All-Blacks' team.

For instance, numerous rugby teams are currently using wearable technology from Catapult Sports. Catapult's technology consists of devices worn on the body by players and collects physiological parameters during training and playing sessions. This is then uploaded to databases where AI algorithms are applied to analyse the data and provide insights on player performance, conditioning and risk of injury to the coaching staff. This information will help the coaching staff make training load and tactical decisions and manage players based on biomechanical insights.

11.4: Conclusion

Its support can cover all aspects of the game, including strategy, play analysis and strength and conditioning. By providing information about how players move, what is happening in play and what opponents are aiming to do, AI will enable teams to make better and more strategic decisions about how to play, improving the game of rugby moving forward. In strength and conditioning, AI can provide personalised training programmes, track how players respond to these prescriptions and identify any injuries before they become problems, ensuring that they remain in top shape. As AI technology continues to develop, the scope and sophistication of its applications in rugby will reach new levels, with the sport engaging in a constant improve cycle, providing real-time solutions for teams striving to excel. By using artificial intelligence tools, more individuals and teams will be able to identify areas for improvement and cultivate themselves into stronger rugby players and enhanced teams.

PART-SIX

TENNIS:

Chapter 12: AI in Tennis

12.1. Precision Play: Using AI to Perfect Serve and Volley Techniques

12.2. Match Analysis: AI-Powered Strategies for Game Day

12.3. Injury Prevention: Leveraging AI for Smarter Training and Recovery

12.4 Conclusion

AI in Tennis

12.1: Precision Play: Using AI to Perfect Serve and Volley Techniques

Tennis is a highly technical game, demanding extreme agility and reflexes from every aspect of the court. Two of the markedly technical techniques allow players to take control of a game, in much the same way that yoga lets you achieve shavasana or the perfect figure-four leglock in wrestling. Hitting an ace to win a point by serving, and how well you can volley to put the other player on the back foot, can win or lose matches. Now AI is changing how both techniques are taught, analysed and perfected, offering every player the benefit of enhanced tools to perfect their game.

For instance, perfecting the serve through digital technology mindfully considers detailed biomechanical analyses. High-speed cameras in combination with motion analysis software track each aspect of the serve motion – from the toss to the twist of the wrist to the follow-through – to gather data points that machine-learning algorithms can use to identify and suggest patterns of optimisation. AI can reveal inconsistencies in the ball toss – a crucial factor in the accurate distance and power of the hit.

Through real-time feedback and corrections, AI helps instil incremental improvements that add up to more powerful and precise serves.

In the case of volleying, too, the AI game is close to the human one. Video analysis of volleys can identify not only where the ball is approaching from, but also its speed, spin and trajectory, which can inform the player how to best anticipate and prepare for the volley, focusing on angles that maximise racket positioning and body alignment, aspects of striking crucial to hitting a ball with the utmost speed on a sharp, precise angle. This can be specific both to a player's style and strengths and weaknesses.

Besides, AI game simulators can set up a series of simulated playing scenarios against AI opponents who can return serve and volley without missing. They make the game harder or easier according to the degree of improvement in the player's skills. Once the players' skill has improved, the AI just moves up a notch and makes the next practice scenario slightly more difficult. With the AI, training can take place even when there is no human partner available to play.

12.2: Match Analysis: AI-Powered Strategies for Game Day

But it influences coaches and players as well. AI will affect not just these stars and others like them, who already augment their personal practice with data-driven tools to improve. It even has the potential to increase team preparation and change strategy before game day for all sports. Think of the relatively simple maths in tennis, a sport where every match is different and carries its own set of challenges and opportunities.

As part of its pre-game analysis, in its greatest context, AI can track how an opponent tends to play, what are their strengths and weaknesses, and where they most like to move on the court, perhaps highlighting a specific playing representational space where the opponent struggles on a particular shot, such as a high-spin serve to the backhand, which tends to lead to an error. AI analysis does not stop at the broad-brushstroke level but can be delivered at the very detailed point-by-point data level, equipping players with tactical insights that can be implemented there and then.

In-match AI tools provide real-time analysis of tactics. Sensors embedded in clothing and equipment generate constant streams of data on physiological parameters and performance feedback. Data feeding into AI algorithms is handled on the fly to suggest modifications, such as changing the position of the serve or a change of rallies as fatigue begins to set in. Players remain at peak effectiveness for as long as possible.

12.3: Injury Prevention: Leveraging AI for Smarter Training and Recovery

It is probably the prevention of injuries using AI that could be the single most important therapeutic intervention in sport where AI can help athletes. Servers and baseline players in tennis must practise serving and hitting tennis balls at full pace thousands of times a year. In the case of serve, it becomes a repetitive motion injury that can end one's tennis career. However, AI – even just predictive analytics and tailored training programmes – can mitigate many of these risks.

With historical data and ongoing performance metrics, an AI model could flag the risk of injury by identifying patterns that suggested potential harm to a player's technique or physical strain. For example, an AI system might identify a player's swing mechanics as an indicator that the player would be at risk of an injury to their rotator cuff in the shoulder. In this case, the system may advise changes in technique, or specific conditioning exercises that target specific weak spots in the body.

AI also helps with recovery. After injury, AI-enabled platforms can track an athlete's rehab, and adapt the work of that athlete's rehabilitation team to match his or her fitness recovery at each stage, making sure an athlete returns to full training only when able, and thus reducing the risk of re-injury.

Each of these chapters presents a high-profile AI innovation that is changing the face of tennis by influencing the way that players train, compete and recover. Utilising tennis players' performance, fatigue and injury indicators in the field might soon be transformed by these innovative AI tools. In turn, this will allow tennis players to improve their performance and engage in the sport for longer periods of time.

12.4: Conclusion to Tennis

AI is starting to change the sport by providing cutting-edge tools for training, competing and recovering. Using AI technologies as part of a daily regimen enables young players to refine virtually every aspect of the game, from learning serve mechanics and volleying technique from motion analysis to creating match simulations for strategic planning. Injury-prevention and recovery protocols also offer the promise of playing longer and healthier careers for those with an intense appetite for the sport. An AI-civilised tennis landscape not only improves facility performance but also democratises access to training tools that have been previously available only to the sport's best players and coaches. Government subsidies, grant funding and corporate sponsorship will continue to be strategic investments.

HOCKEY:

CHAPTER THIRTEEN

AI in Hockey

13.1: AI in Action: Enhancing Stick Handling and Shooting Accuracy

For example, in hockey the ability to stick-handle and shoot is a unique skill, and the key difference between a good player and a great player. The way artificial intelligence (AI) is being used in training regimes is now starting to impact how these skills can be developed and learnt in ways that weren't possible in the past. AI provides specific detail and feedback from many different views at once and allows for personalised coaching that empowers the players to have a deeper and clearer understanding of their performance.

Motion capture and analysis technologies, the very apex of artificial intelligence, are also fundamental to many of these improvements. Players run through stickhandling drills in slow motion, with multiple high-speed cameras capturing and measuring every millimetre of the motion. Every stick position, every player's posture, every movement of the puck through the net is recorded and converted into data. This information is fed to machine-learning algorithms that look for biases and inefficiencies in the player's style. For example, an AI might evaluate whether a player's stick handling is causing them to slow down, or whether it's affecting their balance. Coaches and players can then apply deliberate practice on those specific aspects of their technique.

Additionally, such AI training devices can present the player with in-game situations and allow them to practise their responses in a safe, yet challenging environment such as passing the puck or getting around a defender. For example, VR setups can simulate these high-pressure moments, having a player deal with long and short passing options while being tracked and scored to match their skill level, ultimately helping them improve. AI learns the player and raises or lowers the difficulty and complexity as needed.

It's also increasingly helping to boost shooting accuracy, by analysing video of shooting drills frame-by-frame to check the biomechanics and trajectory of every shot, and to suggest the optimal angles and forces needed to net the puck. Machine-learning research is examining ways to increase accuracy by teaching players to change subtle aspects of their shooting form, such as the position of their wrists relative to the stick. What's more, another use of AI analysis is to record the position of all the pucks, players and goalies in practise and simulation, and to show players how to recognise telltale holes in an opponent's defences.

13.2: Game Strategy Optimization: AI Tools for Analysing Opponent Plays

With an eye to his highly competitive sport, strategic planning and analysis is key as a team looks to game video for keys to their rivals' tactics – and, for that matter, for strategies to use against other teams as well. Pollard notes the AI's capacity to chew through vast amounts of game footage, providing intelligence to teams that's far more detailed than anything a human could track.

Prior to game day, AI systems can ingest historical data on an opponent's squad, preparing individual reports on how they're likely to line up, how they tend to play, and how their players will respond to different situations: a report that allows a coach to tailor a specific counterstrategy. If a team's biggest offensive threat is the rim-shaking, Kwame-esque full-steam power forward Okoye Okiya, a pre-game report showing that Okiya makes 50 per cent of his shots after receiving a pick-and-roll from point guard 'Hot Shot' Legutu, could lead the coach to assign a guard to be aggressive on the pick.

AI-powered real-time analytics can provide dynamic tactics advice for players on the ice in addition to training and injury prediction, AI has the power to improve sports in real-time. Advanced tools that make use of AI algorithms can be used to analyse live data streams, captured by sensors embedded in players' equipment and the puck, which can instantly recognize changes in opposition tactics. This can help in-game coaches make real-time tactical decisions, such as changing line-ups or defensive formations, in response to emerging threats.

Moreover, in the post-game review, AI renders detailed breakdowns of what happened when the team implemented this or that planned strategy. Coaches and players may review this account and think, what worked just now, what didn't, and how do we do it better next time?

13.3: Dynamic Conditioning: AI-Driven Training Programs for Peak Performance

Hockey training involves not just improving fitness but reconditioning it for the specific demands of this sport, and when it comes to developing aerobic and anaerobic conditioning routines that optimise athletic performance and mitigate injury risk, there are no better AI-enabled training programs.

Data gleaned from detailed information on every aspect of an athlete's performance across time – from heart rate to speed, power output to fatigue – is studied to tailor training programmes for the individual; and, as the athlete responds positively to a regime, the AI system modifies it in real time. For instance, if the player appears to be tiring, the system might recommend a lighter training day or day spent focusing on recovery.

Recovery is another area in which AI comes into play, scheduling recovery protocols using data from biometric sensors to help players recover based on their individual physiological needs. Ice baths, massage and stretching can be scheduled at optimal times to facilitate this process and help players arrive at game day ready to perform.

Along the way, the player's training program becomes personalised and programmatic, helping him stay at peak health throughout the season and, if all goes well, giving him the ability to extend his career by keeping him healthier for longer.

 Each of these chapters shows the way that AI is remaking hockey on a team-by-team basis, not only improving individuals' game but also reshaping how teams play and how players train and work out so they can run faster, shoot harder and play better.

13.4: Conclusion to Hockey

AI (artificial intelligence) is having a profound impact on hockey, going far beyond the 'gimmick' zone. It touches everything from a player's individual skill development to how a team attacks, defends and executes tactical strategy. In the cyber world, players using programmes to improve stick handling and shooting technique are sharpening their skills – thereby showing up better on the ice. Coaches creating plays based on analysis of opponent tendencies and actual game-play data enhance their team's on-ice performance. And when AI enables dynamic conditioning with real-time settings to not only enhance performance in the rink but also to minimise the risks of injury, the technology is poised to become an even more important part of training for hockey players of all levels.

PART-EIGHT

BASEBALL:

Chapter 14: AI in Baseball

14.1. Swing Mechanics: AI Techniques for Batting Excellence

14.2. Pitch Prediction: Harnessing AI for Strategic Batting and Pitching

14.3. Defensive Plays: AI Integration for Field Positioning and Play Execution

CHAPTER FOURTEEN

AI in Baseball

14.1: Swing Mechanics: AI Techniques for Batting Excellence

Baseball, a sport rich with tradition, is being revolutionised by artificial intelligence (AI) applied to player training – in particular batting – where an extraordinarily precise series of mechanics is involved in getting a strike. In other words, the bat must meet the ball from the precisely correct angle for this hit to result in a home run. AI is a sophisticated method for measuring, correcting and precisely assessing this swing mechanism.

High-speed cameras and motion-capture technology all feed into the software so that AI systems can learn about and respond to every aspect of the batter's swing: the angle of the bat, the position of the feet, the twist of the hips, the bend of the knees and the follow-through after each swing. In this way, it becomes possible for AI to explain why a certain swing combination might increase power and accuracy, or how minor adjustments might improve performance.

So, if a player is known to sway as he swings, the system can detect that pattern by analysing motion data, and the AI can alert coaches and players. The AI could provide drills to enhance shoulder level by using visual cues and haptic feedback to alter the player's posture consciously or subconsciously in real time. AI could also, for the batter, simulate pitches of all varieties (fastball, curveball, knuckleball) giving the batter a chance to swing at a wide variety of pitches so that he can adjust his timing and swing for all different gaming situations.

Second, overlapping with individual training, AI applications can track and analyse performance data across time, pick out trends and even predict outcomes of future games. Coaches can thus rely on statistical probability of success when picking positions for certain players and when assigning batting order.

14.2: Pitch Prediction: Harnessing AI for Strategic Batting and Pitching

The pitcher-batter duel in baseball – a game of cat and mouse because each player tries to read the other one to counter his or her strategy – is only ever going to be enhanced by AI technology, which can further aid pitch prediction and strategic playing.

Swinging at the first pitch or not, the data that an AI system can glean from entire seasons' worth of information about pitchers (including batted balls, pitch type and speed, spin, results in different counts, etc) can identify patterns and tendencies that might not be obvious to a human. For hitters, knowledge of what type of pitches a pitcher will throw – and will he throw them now? Am I ahead or behind in this count? – allows for a higher rate of good contact.

And likewise, pitchers can use AI to help ply and put away batters by providing information on a batter's profile against their past at-bats. It can recommend the best pitches to throw and the most advantageous spots to locate them. This strategy both improves the pitcher and puts extra psychological pressure on the batter, who must adjust to more intelligently designed pitches.

Moreover, AI can adjust over time by evaluating game-time data and sculpting a strategy on the fly. 'If a pitcher's fast balling is not working well that day, we would have the technology to tell him to start throwing the ball differently. If he's facing an impressive group of hitters, we might have him change the proportion of off-speed pitches.' The fine-grain adjustments that AI can provide are critical in high-stakes games where the momentum can shift with each pitch.

14. 3: Defensive Plays: AI Integration for Field Positioning and Play Execution

While defensive play in baseball is underscored by the individual defence, its effectiveness depends upon team coordination. AI advances defensive activity for the team through advanced data analysis and in-game positioning recommendations.

AI-powered analytics assess the probability of a hit being made to a particular location, based on factors such as the current pitcher, batter and game conditions. Hazards can be modelled prospectively with predictive equipment, allowing AI to recommend optimal defensive positioning to maximise coverage of the field. So if a speed pitch from you is likely to be driven to right field when faced by a particular batter with poor timing, you might be wise to adjust your fielders accordingly.

In an individual capacity, AI improves reaction speeds and decision-making. Infielders, for example, can use simulations and drills that zone in on reacting to ground balls, or on double plays. Timed with the speed of a major-league baseball game, these training tools will help to overcome any scenario in which a player takes too long to react. They use already-collected data from real-game performance to generate countless more simulations. All of this is done to prepare a player for high-leverage situations.

Furthermore, coaches can use AI-powered video review of defensive settings and outcomes to help identify how teams might optimise fielding setups going forward. By remotely replaying moments of defensive setup and responses to individual runners, teams can learn how to optimise their defensive strategies for future games.

Each chapter details the way AI is revolutionising baseball, and how, with an unprecedented resource, players and coaches can perfect their craft, formulate new strategic approaches and hone their execution. As AI becomes increasingly sophisticated, its involvement in baseball is likely to only increase. Baseball is starting to look a lot more like the modern world.

14.4: Conclusion to Baseball

In baseball, AI has quickly become an indispensable part of modern training environments, providing actual feedback to players that they previously couldn't get for themselves about their own swing mechanics, pitch sequences and distribution, game-dependent defensive positioning and actual execution, and more. With AI analysis, players can also see how their batting and pitching tendencies fare well against their opponents' styles and abilities and can therefore target critical areas for quantifiable improvement in their functional training. Even baseball teams can use AI-based dynamic situational analysis to decide the best field setups for any given game condition and situation and can execute plays with the right strategy. AI tools are already ingrained in training activities and game-day strategy planning, and these tools will continue to shape how players train, how coaches' strategies for their teams, and how teams perform on the diamond.

PART-NINE

BASKETBALL:

Chapter 15: AI in Basketball

15.1. Court Vision: AI Applications in Enhancing Shooting and Passing Skills

15.2. Opponent Analysis: Using AI to Develop Defensive Strategies

15.3. Player Fitness: AI-Driven Approaches to Conditioning and Injury Management

15.4 Conclusion

CHAPTER FIFTEEN

AI in Basketball

15.1 Court Vision: AI Applications in Enhancing Shooting and Passing Skills

In a sport where shooting is crucial, success can hinge on millimetre precision and split-second decisions about when to pass to a teammate or not. Artificial intelligence (AI)-driven technologies are changing how real players practice their craft, enabling new analytical approaches to training for greater accuracy and decision-making.

One obvious set of AI capabilities in basketball training is using sophisticated motion capture systems, and analysing data fed into machine learning algorithms to play back shooting mechanics and passing strategies. Take shooting. What was your form like? When did you release the ball in relation to the angle or stride? How was your follow-through? You might have the perfect form, but AI can run the numbers and tell you what slight tweaks you can make, for greater accuracy. Let's imagine you have trouble with shooting a three-pointer in the corner of the field. AI might spot that you could improve your shooting percentage by releasing the ball a few degrees to the right of your shoulder a tenth of a second before leaving your feet and can feed that into the display for you to pick up during practice.

From a passing perspective, this could entail AI helping a player see the 'highest value' options for the passer at any given game state. It could simulate in-game scenarios so the player learning how to pass knows when, where and how to make effective passes based on game conditions. The AI could potentially simulate these scenarios based on self-identified roles and/or team strategies, such that training scenarios are directly transferrable to the AI-authored game state.

Furthermore, machine learning-driven analytics feeds will offer feedback on play outcomes, enabling teams to tweak their offence playbook for better orchestration – from the volley of players on the court to their spacing within the arc or free-throw line, the split-second of passing from one teammate to the next, or the perfected rhythm of a layup.

15. 2: Opponent Analysis: Using AI to Develop Defensive Strategies

Defensive strategy in basketball is essential, not just due to the required agility but also because it entails thinking deeply about the reasons behind opponents' actions. AI plays a key role in its development, since it can offer an in-depth joint explanation of opponents' style of play and their personal tendencies. This means that defending players and their coaches are prepared to disrupt their opponents' offensive techniques in the best possible way by having a thorough understanding of their behaviour.

AIs can comb through games worth of footage to look for tendencies in the way opponents prefer to attack. These might involve specific shots (e.g., three-pointers), geographical areas of the court that they prefer to score in, or the occurrence of certain set plays. For example, knowing that an opponent tends to score three-pointers from a few key zones on the court could lead to a defensive philosophy that attempts to tighten guard pressure on those zones.

It can also track and use the data to learn one player's habits – for example, the way he tends to drive to his left rather than his right. This kind of information is invaluable to a team's defenders, especially if they're able to flood the weak side, or to work more aggressively in the help position. AI is also useful for simulating one-on-one matchups. Analysing past games, AI can present users with all the various ways that a player might defend a specific offensive player, helping them prepare for any kind of offensive assault.

Real-time AI on the sidelines gives coaches the opportunity to make in-game adjustments, including immediately calling for a defensive switch based on AI's interpretation of a live data feed, or alerting the coaching staff to tell the defensive player they're on that matchup that he's getting beaten because he doesn't hold the screen on the pick-and-roll. It can keep your defences at an advantage.

15.3: Player Fitness: AI-Driven Approaches to Conditioning and Injury Management

As a fast and full-contact sport, basketball places great demands on players' fitness, and keeping players in top physical shape is crucial for peak performance. AI can help better manage players' fitness by providing real-time monitoring and predictive analytics to keep the players on the court and minimise injury.

With wearable technology integrated with AI components that continually track players' physiological parameters, the physical demands of playing can be measured, and fatigue-related metrics, e.g., ventricular heart rates, or lower extremity output, can be ascertained during games and in training sessions. AI algorithms based on this telemetry can provide real-time assessments of fatigue status and recovery and permits personnel to tailor everyone's training loads and recovery periods accordingly.

Additionally, injury prevention is another major application in which AI saves the day. Studying on data showing movements, as well as physical responses, AI can detect if there are risk factors for injuries like strains or sprains, which can be addressed earlier and prevent them from occurring in the first place – whether it be altering the intensity of training or focusing on strength and flexibility exercises where there is a higher risk of injury.

Additionally, AI supports more efficient and targeted rehabilitation processes, which recommend training and exercise programmes according to the individual needs and recovery status of sportspeople. In doing so, the technology not only enables earlier return dates but also reduces the risk of re-injury, thus supporting athletes in a longer, healthier sporting career.

Every chapter tells how AI is changing basketball in diverse ways – from developing core skills to assessing the opposition, from decision-making and pattern recognition to managing player health and performance. As AI technology advances, its utility in basketball is set to grow, but also promises new opportunities for making the game even better and players even more effective.

15.4: Conclusion to Basketball

Basketball ranking Instructions: With its rapid pace and complex strategic tenets, basketball seems a logical choice for artificial integration. AI, at present, helps individual players enhance their shooting, passing, and dribbling abilities. Moreover, AI can help teams adopt optimal defensive setups to counter strategic threats from opponents. For example, when an offence tends to steer towards one side of the court, certain AI systems can help coaches organise defensive positions to create traps, pushing the ball handler out of bounds or drawing fouls. Similarly, AI can, in the future, help fitness trainers create programmes to achieve optimal player fitness. While some of the practical applications help human players gain an edge over their opponents in field situations, others facilitate the collation and processing of data to adopt a reflective stance in the sport, which also make it more inclusionary. For instance, if coaches identify certain types of plays that an opposing team tends to play with greater frequency or efficiency, they may use automated AI systems to predict player movements during those plays and adopt more optimal strategies in the future. However, contemporary uses of AI are not limited to basketball alone. To add another dimension to the game, AI can also help create digital archetypes of various scenarios that regular spectators in stadiums can actively participate in.

VOLLEYBALL:

CHAPTER SIXTEEN

AI in Volleyball

16.1 AI-Assisted Serve and Attack Formations: Training for Power and Precision

Volleyball, a sport defined by precision and power, requires rigorous training and strategic acumen to master its complex dynamics. AI technology is increasingly utilized to enhance these aspects, particularly in serving and attacking, which are pivotal elements of the game. AI offers sophisticated tools that can improve accuracy and power, tailor training, and optimize strategic formations based on real-time data analysis.

AI-driven training systems use motion capture technology to analyse and refine a player's serving and spiking techniques. These systems record detailed biomechanical data, such as arm swing speed, angle of approach, and point of contact with the ball. Advanced algorithms process this data to identify inefficiencies and suggest modifications to improve both power and accuracy. For instance, AI might recommend adjustments in the timing of the jump or the angle of the wrist upon contact, which can significantly enhance the effectiveness of serves and attacks.

Furthermore, AI can simulate different in-game scenarios to help players practice their serves and spikes under various conditions. These simulations can be programmed to mimic the defensive setups that players are likely to encounter in matches, allowing them to develop adaptive strategies and improve their decision-making under pressure. The ability to train against virtual opponents designed to challenge specific weaknesses is invaluable in preparing players for competitive play.

In addition to individual skills, AI assists coaches in designing effective serve and attack formations. By analysing data from past matches, AI can suggest strategic placements and sequences that maximize the team's scoring potential while exploiting the opponent's vulnerabilities. This level of strategic planning is crucial for high-level volleyball, where the proper formation can disrupt the opponent's defence and open up opportunities for scoring.

16.2 Defensive Structures: AI Insights for Improving Block and Dig Techniques

Defence in volleyball is as critical as offense, involving coordinated team effort and individual prowess in blocking and digging. AI technology enhances defensive training by providing insights into optimal positioning, timing, and technique, tailored to counter specific offensive threats posed by opponents.

Using machine learning models, AI analyses video footage from matches to study opponents' attacking patterns, identifying common routes and tactics used in spikes. This information allows defensive players to anticipate where to position themselves to effectively block or dig an incoming attack. For example, AI can detect a tendency for an opponent to favour attacks from the right flank and advise adjustments in the defensive lineup to strengthen that area.

AI also helps in refining the technical aspects of blocking and digging. By reviewing performance data, AI can offer feedback on a player's reaction time, jump height, and hand positioning during a block. For digs, AI can evaluate the player's stance, footwork, and the angle of arm contact, providing precise recommendations for improvement. Training sessions augmented by AI feedback ensure that players are not only reacting instinctively but also applying the most effective techniques to neutralize the attack.

Moreover, AI-driven tools can create highly realistic training simulations that mimic the offensive strategies of upcoming opponents. This hands-on practice allows players to experience firsthand the speed and complexity of the attacks they will face, preparing them mentally and physically for actual game situations.

16.3 Performance Analytics: Using AI for Tactical Team Arrangement and Rotation

Strategic team arrangement and player rotation are critical components in volleyball that significantly impact the outcome of a game. AI's capability to process and analyse extensive data provides coaches with a strategic edge, enabling them to make informed decisions about player positioning and rotation.

AI systems compile and analyse performance metrics from both individual players and the team. This includes data on serve success rates, attack points, block effectiveness, and more. By evaluating these metrics, AI can identify strengths and weaknesses within the team, suggesting optimal lineup configurations that maximize collective performance and minimize vulnerabilities.

During matches, AI can offer real-time analytics that inform decisions on player rotations and substitutions. For instance, if an AI system observes that a particular player's performance is declining—potentially due to fatigue—it can recommend a substitution to maintain the team's competitive edge. Similarly, AI can suggest tactical shifts in player positions based on the flow of the game and the effectiveness of current strategies.

Additionally, AI tools facilitate post-match analysis by providing detailed breakdowns of how different team arrangements and rotations performed. This ongoing evaluation helps refine future strategies, ensuring that teams are continually learning and adapting their tactics to be more effective in subsequent games.

In each of these chapters, AI stands out as a transformative tool in volleyball, enhancing training, refining techniques, and elevating strategic gameplay. As technology continues to advance, the integration of AI in volleyball promises even greater advancements, enabling players and teams to achieve new heights of performance.

16.4 Conclusion to Volleyball

Volleyball players and coaches who are equipped with AI technologies have a clear advantage over their non-AI counterparts. Not only does AI help enhance volleyball skill, such as serving, spiking and blocking, it also empowers coaches to provide higher-quality feedback and enhance strategic decision-making (e.g., defensive allocations and team line-up). For example, with AI's feedback, a player can improve her spiking accuracy by practising in a simulated game that provides a highly realistic and controllable training environment. In addition to training, the strategic insights provided by AI can also help volleyball players devise smarter game plans and make more effective in-match adjustments. With AI investments, volleyball might eventually become as professional and precise as basketball. When the era of volleyball AI comes, it could help visually impaired volleyball become a successful professional sport. It might even inspire a surge of new players who are passionate about both volleyball and technology.

GOLF:

CHAPTER SEVENTEEN

AI in GOLF

17.1: Driving Success: AI-Enhanced Techniques for Mastering the Tee Shot

The tee shot sets the tone for the whole hole; if you don't get a decent tee shot, the rest of your approach is going to be much more difficult. And the thing about the tee shot is that young players are trying for more distance. The big hitters play the courses the rest of us play on a much shorter par, and it becomes much easier to get the ball into the hole with fewer strokes – it's the importance of driving, which is really the heart of the game. Today, artificial intelligence (AI) can be built into the technique that helps young golfers hit further and straighter. It can even tell you important details about your swings.

A high-speed camera and sensors pick up every twitch of a golfer's tee shot, including swing speed, launch angle, spin rates and club path. Then algorithmic analytical devices calculate and report deviations from ideal mechanics, and pinpoint patterns and adjustments. If you have a tendency to have the clubface open at impact – if your hands are too far away from your body at the end of the swing – AI devices will pick up on this and connect you with information to help you hold the clubface square at impact – or modify your swing to get the ball into the fairway.

What's more, golfers could use AI-driven simulators to practice tee shots in a variety of conditions – high wind, low clouds, shade, sun – even in an empty space the size of a bedroom, without the need for expansive driving ranges. AI-powered simulators can simulate dedicated areas at the driving range of a course, offer different course layouts, mimic high-pressure scenarios and calibrate the difficulty of challenges and different kinds of feedback according to each player's ability and progress level.

Instead of just helping with individual shots, the AI can help craft personalised training programmes that hone in on particular weaknesses. Could low launch angles be the player's Achilles heel? The data would be used to help devise physical exercises and drills that would help the client strengthen the right muscles.

17.2: Precision Putting: Using AI to Refine Your Short Game

Putting is often how golf matches are won and lost, so precise execution on the short game is crucial. Here, AI technologies offer detailed side-by-side analyses of putting strokes and virtual replicas of the greens for building muscle memory and putting skills. As players gain confidence through AI-supported data-driven insights and digital, virtual, and repeatable practice scenarios, they home in on distance, direction, and surface analysis.

Sensors and cameras positioned in AI-augmented putting greens can monitor, in extraordinarily precise detail, the way each ball rolls and the mechanics of each putting stroke. Thanks to feedback on parameters as minute as the stroke path, the face angle of the head at impact and the speed the ball was putted, a putting stroke can be modified to perfection by the tiniest of tweaks, sometimes the difference between holing out and not.

Virtual reality (VR), a more sophisticated version of this idea, takes golf practice to another level by letting players practice their putting on digitally promoted recreations of real-world greens. By altering the variables – the slope and firmness of each green – AI in the VR system will give players putting experiences that vary from green to green. This builds not just skill but confidence as players learn how to change their strokes according to the demands of the green.

But AI can assist in the cognitive elements of putting as well, such as judging distances and green-reading via pattern-recognition technologies (a sensible technique that gobs alongside pressure strokes and initial putts, which in turn are influenced by putting style). It can also be used to help players better discern green breaks and slopes that they otherwise might not see, preparing the golfer to address a putt understanding how the ball will move.

17.3: Course Management and Strategic Play: AI Insights for Every Hole

Engaging course management to play to the strength and weakness of each hole is necessary, and AI will excel at drawing on copious amounts of data from multiple holes and the various courses presenting the challenges to guide strategic skills and championship decision-making which extend from club selection to shot selection, all the way down to the type of shot one is to play.

Historical performance data such as approach shot distances and putts per green can be analysed by AI systems, which can then advise on how to play the hole. For instance, based on the hole layout, wind conditions and locations of hazards, an AI model might suggest a play strategy (eg, fade the ball around a bunker) for each hole. Such advisement, based on the wisdom of many past golfers, can be incredibly useful to a beginner or someone in their 20s and 30s. The AI system appears to know as much about the course as a 60-something lifelong player.

In addition, suggestions can be adjusted on the fly, based on how a player is performing in real time during the course of a round. If a player is flying it and racking up some extra yards on drives, it could suggest going for the green on the next par 5. Or, if AI were to notice that a player didn't quite have his drive straight that day, it might suggest conservative strategies to pick up some keystrokes.

17.4: Injury Prevention and Swing Analysis: Leveraging AI for Safer, More Effective Practice

Another aspect in which AI plays a key part in injury prevention is by studying a player's swing mechanics to alert them if any aspects of their game could result in injuries. Since golf involves a chain of similar motions, repeating the same swing hundreds of times every round, delicate parts of the body can be strained and even develop injuries over time. With the help of AI, motion-capture imagery and biomechanics, a golfer can identify risky aspects of their game and promote good posture and alignment to ensure that they avoid straining their body and exposing themselves to potential injury.

Photo-or video-analysis systems based on AI track a golfer's kinematics during the swing, turning points that generate excessive strain on joints or muscles into actionable feedback. For instance, say a player's shoulder alignment causes her to put unnecessary strain on her lower back; here, AI can draw attention to the problem, and suggest biomechanical adjustments of her swing or a course of specific conditioning exercises to mitigate the risk of an injury.

In addition to this, AI can measure the player's fatigue levels during training sessions and allow adjustment to the training regimen on the spot by, for example, authorising a break or a different training regime that day. This is another example of how Mongovision, which emphasises the importance of training safety and longevity in the sport, differs from the current paradigm of golf.

AI training could help young golfers to develop not only terms of the technicalities but overall the health and strategy so that they could play for much longer and enjoy it even more These responses clearly show that while the ultimate outcome of golf might remain the same, having a supportive mentor to embrace the use of AI in training could help young golfers to develop not only the technical elements but overall the health and strategy so that they could play for much longer and enjoy it even more. This is precisely the type of development we need in order to maximise the potential of young golfers in the long term, and most importantly, enhance their enjoyment of the game.

GENERAL SPORTS TRAINING:

CHAPTER EIGHTEEN

Data-Driven Training: Leveraging Big Data for Performance Enhancement

18.1 Collecting and Analysing Performance Data

The saying 'Knowledge is power' has likely never been truer than it is now in the age of data-driven training. Using big data to enhance performance is a rising trend in most sports and giving coaches and athletes an edge in competition by increasing their understanding of dexterity metrics, training efficiency and injury prevention is a game-changer.

The first step in data-driven training is the collection of performance data. Performance data can be collected using a whole slew of wearable devices, GPS trackers, heart rate monitors or advanced video analysis systems. Smart watches and fitness bands using wearable technology can measure all sorts of cardiac and other physiological metrics such as heart rate, distance travelled, speed, number of paces or steps, and so on. GPS trackers can be useful in soccer and rugby, where you can track the distance travelled by each player, speed, acceleration and deceleration, and even visualise this over space and time as three-dimensional positional heat maps.

Video analysis systems employing high-definition cameras and computer-vision algorithms allow coaches to analyse a player's motions frame-by-frame in real time. This level of detail allows coaches to evaluate an athlete's technique from a granular approach when functionally breaking down the components, such as running form or shot mechanics, and help to find areas of subtle biomechanical inefficiencies if a player isn't technically sound or if there's a risk of injuries.

Finally, the data needs to be understood, which involves running algorithms capable of inferring meaning from patterns and correlations otherwise invisible to the human eye. A stark example of big data analytics in action comes from the world of sport. Machine learning models can process performance data to discern if an athlete has increased his or her chances of injury based on previous workloads, recovery micro cycles and biomechanical metrics. Such predictive analytics are invaluable – how else could you design training programmes to get the most out of an athlete while ensuring that he or she remains healthy and performs at their peak?

18.2 Customizing Training Programs Based on Data Insights

Among these, perhaps the most important advantage of data-driven training is that it is not based on previous success and failure of Olympians or players, but on a particular athlete's weakness, experience and other related factors that can be accounted for when creating a training plan that benefits them directly. Possibly the biggest concern that people have about the growing use of data in training is the fact that, at least for now, human brains are still better than algorithms at certain components of decision-making in sports.

Trainers can use those metrics to pinpoint the exact aspects of a performance that need tuning up. A sprinter might see in their data that their acceleration phase is slower than their top speed phase, and so the coach would be able to create drills and exercises designed to focus on the specific needs of dealing with that explosive acceleration off the blocks. As for the basketball player, if data shows he or she shoots at 95 per cent accuracy but under fatigue that drops to 70 per cent, a trainer could then programme a training session that has the player shooting at high intensity during periods of fatigue.

Furthermore, data-driven training can be used to individualise training loads. Athletes who overtrain at too high an intensity risk burnout and injury; data analytics can be used to continually monitor heart-rate variability, sleep quality and post-training soreness, and provide feedback to the coach in real time to manage pre-announced training loads dynamically throughout the season.

Finally, optimising training programmes is a big part of what's required to become a pro; excellence is rare, and the only way to achieve it is through systematic training. Periodisation, or the systematic planning of athletic training, can be made more effective with data. We can use research-based data on runner replenishment to design periodised training plans that help athletes perform best over the course of the season: for example, if we know from performance data that an athlete works best during certain times of a day, week or season within a season, we can use this information to structure training cycles so that they peak at the right times. For example, when training an athlete for major competitions or playoffs, coaches will optimise performance so that athletes peak at the right times.

When it comes to team sports, predictive analytics can also help with tactical preparation: training regimens can be built to better suit the players, and matchup data can reveal weaknesses in the opposing team. Predictive analysis in soccer, for instance, can help a coach spot the unique tendencies of an opponent's defensive formations, suggesting a better plan of attack; the same can be done in basketball, unpicking the ways in which opposing teams behave.

18.3 Conclusion

Data-driven training represents a new wave of training concepts, where recent advances in collecting and analysing performance data are providing athletes and coaches with a granular insight into what drives success. Such a flood of information allows for the customisation of training sets for the needs of each athlete, optimising his/her performance while reducing the risk of injury. And there is no reason to doubt that big data will not continue helping the future generation of athletes to improve their skills through more sophisticated tools and methodologies. In other words, big data is becoming an integral part of the standard sports training to a point that it might easily become the new expectation that the sports culture should be based on science and evidence. Such a shift towards a more scientific approach to sports training promises to lift athletic and competition standards to even greater heights across all sports.

CHAPTER NINETEEN

Injury Prevention and Recovery with AI

Athletes sustain injuries, many of which are now treated with artificial intelligence. Numerous companies are exploring new approaches to either preventing injuries or optimising the recovering process. One application of predictive analytics in AI involves identifying the risk factors that can lead to injury, while another optimises recovery processes in the aftermath of athletic trauma. Thanks to AI, athletic performance is enhanced, and careers extended.

19.1 Identifying Risk Factors and Preventing Injuries

Preventing injuries begins with understanding the risk factors that predispose athletes to them. AI excels in analysing vast amounts of data to identify these factors with unprecedented accuracy. Wearable technology, such as smartwatches, fitness trackers, and smart clothing, collects continuous data on an athlete's biomechanics, physical load, and physiological responses. This data includes metrics like heart rate variability, muscle strain, joint angles, and movement patterns.

Machine learning algorithms process this data to detect patterns that indicate an increased risk of injury. For example, an AI system might identify that a soccer player is at higher risk of a hamstring injury due to a combination of factors such as high training loads, insufficient recovery time, and a specific gait pattern. By recognizing these early warning signs, coaches and medical staff can intervene proactively.

Moreover, AI can conduct comparative analyses using historical data from other athletes. For instance, by analysing thousands of injury cases, AI can determine common precursors to specific injuries, such as ACL tears in basketball players. This allows for the development of targeted prevention programs. Personalized training adjustments, such as modifying running techniques, altering training intensity, or incorporating specific strength and flexibility exercises, can then be implemented to mitigate these risks.

AI also plays a crucial role in monitoring fatigue and workload. Over-training is a significant risk factor for injuries, and AI-driven systems can help balance training loads. By continuously monitoring an athlete's workload and recovery metrics, AI can recommend optimal training intensities and rest periods. This ensures athletes are neither undertrained nor overtrained, both of which can lead to injuries.

19.2 Optimizing Recovery Processes through AI

Once an injury occurs, efficient and effective recovery is paramount. AI enhances the recovery process by providing personalized rehabilitation programs, monitoring progress, and making data-driven adjustments to treatment plans.

One of the key applications of AI in recovery is in the creation of individualized rehabilitation plans. Traditional rehab protocols often follow a standardized approach, which may not be suitable for every athlete. AI can analyse an athlete's specific injury details, medical history, and recovery data to design a tailored rehabilitation plan. For example, after an ACL surgery, AI can recommend specific exercises, intensity levels, and progression timelines that are best suited to the individual's recovery rate and overall physical condition.

AI-driven rehabilitation programs often incorporate biofeedback mechanisms, where real-time data on the athlete's performance during rehab exercises is collected and analysed. Wearable sensors can track movement accuracy, range of motion, and muscle activation. AI algorithms compare this data against desired performance metrics, providing immediate feedback to the athlete and therapist. This ensures exercises are performed correctly and effectively, minimizing the risk of re-injury and speeding up recovery.

Additionally, AI can optimize recovery through virtual coaching and telemedicine. Virtual reality (VR) and augmented reality (AR) platforms guided by AI can simulate interactive rehab sessions, allowing athletes to perform exercises with virtual coaches who provide real-time corrections and encouragement. This is particularly beneficial for athletes who may not have continuous access to physical therapists.

AI also enhances recovery by predicting optimal return-to-play timelines. Using data from previous injuries and recoveries, AI can provide evidence-based estimates of when an athlete is likely to be ready to return to full competition. This helps in managing expectations and reduces the risk of premature return, which could lead to re-injury.

In terms of ongoing monitoring, AI systems can track recovery progress through regular assessments of physical and physiological parameters. By continuously updating the recovery plan based on real-time data, AI ensures that the rehabilitation process remains dynamic and responsive to the athlete's needs.

19.3 Conclusion

The integration of AI in injury prevention and recovery is transforming sports medicine. By identifying risk factors through detailed data analysis, AI helps prevent injuries before they occur. When injuries do happen, AI optimizes the recovery process with personalized rehabilitation plans, real-time monitoring, and adaptive treatment adjustments. This not only accelerates recovery but also enhances long-term athletic performance and career longevity. As AI technology continues to evolve, its role in injury prevention and recovery will undoubtedly expand, offering even more sophisticated and effective solutions for athletes.

CHAPTER TWENTY

Mental Toughness and AI: Building the Athlete's Mindset

Mental toughness is a crucial attribute for athletes, enabling them to perform consistently under pressure, maintain focus, and overcome setbacks. AI is increasingly being utilized to enhance mental resilience, offering innovative tools and techniques to build a robust athlete's mindset. By leveraging AI, athletes can develop mental toughness through personalized training programs, visualization, and focus techniques.

20.1 Using AI to Enhance Mental Resilience

Mental resilience is the ability to adapt to stress and adversity, maintaining a positive and focused mindset. AI-driven platforms can enhance mental resilience by providing personalized psychological training programs tailored to an athlete's specific needs.

AI can analyse data from various sources, such as performance metrics, psychological assessments, and even social media interactions, to identify factors that affect an athlete's mental state. For instance, natural language processing (NLP) algorithms can analyse text and speech patterns to detect signs of stress, anxiety, or confidence levels. By understanding these psychological indicators, AI can recommend targeted interventions to address specific mental challenges.

One application of AI in building mental resilience is through biofeedback mechanisms. Wearable devices that monitor physiological responses, such as heart rate variability, galvanic skin response, and brainwave activity, can provide real-time feedback on an athlete's stress levels. AI algorithms analyse this data and suggest relaxation techniques, breathing exercises, or mindfulness practices to help athletes manage stress and maintain composure.

Moreover, AI-driven virtual coaches can offer personalized mental resilience training programs. These programs might include cognitive-behavioural techniques, stress management strategies, and goal-setting exercises. By providing continuous support and adaptive feedback, virtual coaches help athletes build a strong mental foundation, enabling them to stay focused and confident in high-pressure situations.

20.2 Visualization and Focus Techniques

Visualization is a powerful mental technique that involves creating vivid mental images of successful performance. It helps athletes mentally rehearse their skills, strategies, and responses, enhancing their ability to execute them in real-life scenarios. AI can take visualization training to the next level by creating immersive and interactive experiences.

Virtual reality (VR) and augmented reality (AR) platforms powered by AI can simulate realistic game situations, allowing athletes to practice their visualization techniques in a controlled and immersive environment. For example, a basketball player can use VR to visualize making free throws in a crowded and noisy arena, helping them build confidence and focus. AI algorithms can customize these simulations based on the athlete's performance data, ensuring that the visualization exercises are challenging and relevant.

AI can also enhance focus techniques by providing personalized attention training. Attention training involves exercises that improve an athlete's ability to concentrate on relevant stimuli while ignoring distractions. AI-driven attention training programs can analyse an athlete's focus patterns and provide targeted exercises to improve concentration. For instance, AI can create interactive games that require athletes to track multiple moving objects or respond to specific cues, training their brain to maintain focus in dynamic environments.

Furthermore, AI can assist in developing pre-performance routines that incorporate visualization and focus techniques. These routines help athletes establish a mental framework for optimal performance. AI can analyse data on an athlete's performance during different routines and identify the most effective strategies. For example, an AI system might recommend a specific sequence of visualization exercises, breathing techniques, and motivational self-talk that has been shown to improve performance in previous competitions.

Another innovative application of AI in mental toughness training is the use of neurofeedback. Neurofeedback involves training the brain to achieve desired mental states by providing real-time feedback on brainwave activity. AI algorithms can interpret brainwave data and guide athletes through exercises that promote optimal brain function, such as achieving a calm and focused state. Over time, athletes learn to control their brain activity, enhancing their ability to stay composed and perform under pressure.

20.3 Conclusion

AI is revolutionizing the way athletes build mental toughness, providing advanced tools and techniques to enhance mental resilience, visualization, and focus. By leveraging AI-driven platforms, athletes can receive personalized psychological training, biofeedback, and virtual coaching to strengthen their mental game. Visualization and focus techniques powered by AI, such as VR simulations, attention training, and neurofeedback, offer immersive and interactive experiences that prepare athletes for high-pressure situations. As AI technology continues to evolve, its applications in mental toughness training will expand, offering even more sophisticated and effective solutions to help athletes achieve peak performance and maintain a strong, resilient mindset.

PART-THIRTEEN

FUTURE TRENDS AND ETHICAL CONSIDERATIONS:

CHAPTER TWENTY-ONE

The Future of AI in Sports: Emerging Technologies and Innovations

Significant developments in artificial intelligence (AI) are reshaping the sphere of sports training and performance at a tremendous rate. It is not hard to imagine developments on the horizon as technological capabilities continue to evolve and a number of emerging trends and innovations in AI specifically are already poised to foment significant changes in how athletes train, compete and raise their game. Of course, these changes also set the stage for ethical conundrums that, in turn, will require serious consideration if sports for athletes are to remain as fair as they now are.

21.1 Upcoming Trends and Technologies in AI Sports Training

21.1.1. Enhanced Wearable Technology and Biometric Sensors:

Biometric sensors are already being worn by athletes to monitor training and ailments, and more sophisticated versions will deliver real-time data on body parameters such as muscle fatigue, hydration, blood oxygenation, and even metabolic rates. With the help of AI analysis, this information could give athletes a deeper understanding of their training and recovery processes, allowing them to maximise both.

21.1.2. AI-Powered Injury Prevention and Rehabilitation:

AI injury-prevention and rehabilitation tools: improved precision thanks to better prediction of injury risks (using biomechanics, training loads and historical data), and constantly updated recovery plans based on the athlete's responses and feedback will contribute to shorter recuperation times and lower re-injury risk.

21.1.3. Virtual and Augmented Reality (VR/AR) Training:

At the same time, VR and AR technologies are evolving to become more integral to the training regimen. Athletes will be able to train in VR environments that replicate real-life conditions for their discipline, practising in a virtual arena that they will compete in at the actual game. AR will be able to provide athletes with tactical overlays in real time during their practice session. AR can help athletes make better game-time decisions and therefore help in honing their game further – especially for sports that require in-game strategy, like football, basketball and rugby.

21.1.4. Advanced Performance Analytics:

Performance analytics is set to get even better with AI. It will provide ever more thorough insights into an athlete's strengths and weaknesses. By using algorithms, vast data from video footage, biometrics and gaming statistics can be mined, producing performance reports for coaches, who will be able to design even better training programmes or make even better decisions during a game. With AI, scouting and talent identification will more easily produce objective lists of the best athletes.

21.1.5. Neurofeedback and Cognitive Training:

AI-driven neurofeedback systems will be used to optimise cognitive training for athletes, providing them with information on their brainwave activity and helping them achieve optimal mental states for performance, such as increased focus or relaxation. AI-powered cognitive training programmes will offer personalised mental training exercises to improve mental resilience, decision-making and reaction times. This will be particularly relevant to sporting activities, where mental agility, cognitive processing speed and the ability to quickly react in challenging and pressure-filled situations is vital to driving competitive success.

21.2 Potential Impact on Various Sports Disciplines

How will these emerging AI technologies affect different sports disciplines? For all of us, the outcome will be revolutionary.

21.2.1. Team Sports:

For team sports such as football, basketball and rugby, tactical training and game planning will be radically improved through AI. Analytics on both team and individual players' performances, and how their opponents play, will allow coaches to develop better game plans. Real-time logging and analysis will enable them to tweak tactics during a game to improve performance. Coaches and trainers will also be able to use AI to help manage their players' workloads and to reduce training time, lowering the risk of overtraining and injuries.

21.2.2. Individual Sports:

Fundamental to all these fields will be the use of AI to provide personalised, adaptive training programmes for individuals, whether they are engaged in team or individual sports like tennis, golf, athletics or competitive swimming. Neurofeedback systems will be used to improve mental preparation and biomechanical models of skill will be used to refine technique. VR to practice situations might be applied to practice competitions or to learn new skills. In these latter areas, the 'machine' or device learning aspect will play a significant role, as it will use more data to help athletes adapt to their specific conditions. AI might learn to create moves when playing against another player, just as humans do. In these situations, AI will be able to respond intuitively and spontaneously.

21.2.3. Endurance Sports:

In the case of endurance sports, such as marathon running or cycling, AI will enhance training regimes and recovery strategies to enable optimal performance. Sensor-driven wearables will offer instant physiological feedback on athlete status, enabling real-time, rapid adjustments to training intensity and nutrition to maximise performance. Performance analytics developed by AI enhancements will provide detailed training feedback, enabling athletes to better track their progress and make informed decisions to improve their subsequent training plans. Endurance and efficiency advantage here, too.

21.2.4. Combat Sports:

For sports such as boxing, mixed martial arts or fencing, AI will support refining competitor technique and devising strategy. AI-based video analysis tools will divide up an athlete's actions and determine areas for improvement. Augmented environments will simulate games and competitions against different virtual opponents, allowing athletes to train and test different tactics and skills. AI could also support athlete monitoring to predict injury risks and develop optimal recovery protocols.

CHAPTER TWENTY-TWO

Ethical Considerations and Challenges of AI in Sports

AI has arrived in sports, with significant impacts on training, game play, injury prevention and performance measurement. While league athletic directors have sought guidance for the future of the game, introducing artificial intelligence requires deliberate introspection and a commitment to adhering to the essence of sports (ie, fairness, dignity and skill). Moreover, it carries with it a host of ethical considerations and challenges, such as safeguarding athletes and the sport, ensuring data privacy and safe data collection and storage, and mitigating the creeping dominance of AI to compete or surpass the human mind. To maintain ethical and legal principles in sports, key ethical considerations and their proposed solutions must be met. We urge sports stakeholders to consider these needs as AI progresses in sports.

22.1 Privacy and Data Security

So, while AI is becoming omnipresent in sports, gathering enormous amounts of data (biometric data, performance data, personal data) from athletes, on and off the field, that data inevitably has incredible value not only in terms of training and improving performance but also about other potential – concerning – uses.

22.1.1. Data Ownership and Consent:

An overarching ethical concern is data ownership: athletes must have a clear sense of ownership about their data, as well as ownership of how it is used. This includes gathering informed consent: athletes must know what data is being collected, how it will be used, and by whom. Clear consent processes confirm that athletes' autonomy is being respected.

22.1.2. Data Protection:

High-quality data protections should help to prevent access to sensitive data without authorisation, or its misuse if it is accessed. We therefore encourage monitoring of how organisations (controlling the data) and technology providers proactively apply cybersecurity measures to protect athlete data. These efforts may include encryption, secure storage, and security audits to further protect the data from unauthorised disclosures.

22.1.3. Anonymization and De-identification:

For example, data should be anonymised or de-identified whenever possible so that individual athletes cannot be identified. This means that personal identifiable information such as their name, race, height, weight, city, nationality and other information that could be used to identify an individual is removed from the data set. Anonymisation techniques allow for broad data analysis, while also maintaining personal privacy.

22.1.4. Third-Party Access and Data Sharing:

While athletes and research partners have a right to access the data they generate, sharing with third parties must be regulated. Policies and agreements need to define how data can be shared, with whom, and for what purposes. Athletes should also have explicit consent for any arrangements.

22.1.5. Legal and Regulatory Compliance:

Adherence to legal and binding regulations, such as the General Data Protection Regulation (GDPR) within the European Union, which govern data collection, processing and retention, is also paramount, to ensure that the rights of athletes are safeguarded. Sports organisations must keep up to date with the ever-evolving relevant legislation, and that their practices conform to existing legal frameworks.

22.2 Balancing Human Intuition and AI Assistance:

For all the potential good that AI presents in the sporting sphere, we must guard against a technology-driven encroachment on human judgment, imagination and emotional openness that are so fundamental to sport.

22.2.1. Human-AI Collaboration:

Instead, the aim is to create a conversation between man and machine: a tool for coaches and athletes to enhance human judgement, rather than replace it. AI can tell you what to do, but it can't tell you why. Understanding that 'why' requires human intuition, context and experience – all of which are needed to determine whether an AI decision should in fact constitute a particular course of action. For instance, AI might predict that a certain training regimen is appropriate based on certain performance datapoints. Yet the coach's ability to understand the motivations and mental health of the athlete, as well as her knowledge of a unique set of circumstances, could be key to formulating the regimen in a way that applies the AI insights.

22.2.2 Maintaining Creativity and Adaptability:

Although creative, he's just an actor playing a role. Incidents like the above question the sense in which we apply the word 'athlete' to machines. It's not just creativity that's missing – it's flexibility. Athletes and coaches are constantly taking decisions – often in rapid succession; during groups of games in football, for example, coaches might make as many as four or five different changes to their starting line-up in quick succession. They must think on their feet, adapt what they're doing to changing circumstances, and be creative about how they approach the next minute of play, let alone the next week or month. AI can track past performance, analyse it and predict what will work. But it can't emulate the unpredictable nature of sport. Encouraging athletes to use it might take away the pressure for creativity.

22.2.3. Ethical Decision-Making:

While data and predictive algorithms might be relevant to sporting ethics, and indeed to sport more generally, ethical decision-making in sport cannot be reduced to data and algorithms. Consideration of issues such as training, competition and athlete welfare all depend upon moral and ethical concerns, the resolution of which demands human judgment. For instance, whether an injured athlete should be allowed to continue competing could fuse sporting with medical ethics: that decision might depend on whether the athlete can continue without putting themselves at risk of future injury, the prognosis for the injury, whether the athlete has any chance of winning, and the team's prospects in the competition.

22.2.4. Emotional and Psychological Support:

Unlike an AI, a human coach/support staff can offer up the emotional and psychological support that a human-athlete interaction requires. This ranges from motivating an athlete, to building their confidence, to discussing their emotional needs. An AI might be able to provide a lot more data, but it can't offer the same levels of empathy or connection.

22.2.5. Bias and Fairness:

Third, because AI systems can perpetuate or introduce the biases of the data they're trained on, ensuring fairness and avoiding discriminatory effects will require ongoing monitoring and tuning of AI algorithms. It will be up to human overseers to ferret out those biases, such that sport AI is properly democratised and not inherently discriminatory.

22.3 Conclusion

The use of AI in sports has great potential to aid in performance, training and injury prevention, but it also raises systemic ethical issues that need to be addressed to ensure the fair use of AI technologies. The use of AI should be coupled with ethical protection, privacy and data security, protection of intellectual property, and safeguards such as robust data protection, explicit terms of data ownership, informed consent and ensuring the potential of AI supplements human (intuitive, creative and emotional intelligence) decision-making in the field of sports.

CONCLUSION:

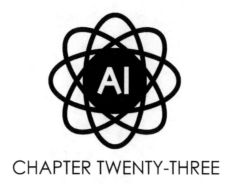

CHAPTER TWENTY-THREE

Harnessing AI for Excellence: A Comprehensive Guide for Young Athletes

Thus, in its role in the sporting transformation, AI becomes a game changer in terms of supporting athletes with optimising their game, training, injuries, diagnosis and rehabilitation, long before it becomes popular with the wholesale generation of synthetic biology athletes and, thereafter, the hordes of AI-empowered autonomous human competitors in our near future. In closing, the goal of this paper has been to expose young athletes to the inevitability of AI in sports and give them an action plan for pre-empting their competitors, helping them to benefit as early in the process as possible, so that they can optimise their game, remain competitive and eventually, win and be champions in whichever field they decide to pursue. This game will continue to evolve rapidly, with new technologies opening new opportunities, requiring new rules. As such, this paper is conceived of as a living document that will be updated, potentially daily, as major developments take place.7

23.1 Summarizing Key Insights and Actionable Steps

23.1.1. Personalized Training Programs:

One of the more important advantages of artificial intelligence is the capacity to develop training regimens that allow for individual, highly customised training. Through the analysis of individual performance data, AI can design training regimens especially for that individual's skill sets and goals. This enables athletes to enhance and maximise their strengths while also ensuring that they address their weaknesses, so that the training itself is conducted in the most efficient manner possible.

23.1.2. Enhanced Performance Analysis:

Powered by artificial intelligence (AI), performance tools such as video analysis and biometric data allow athletes to break down their techniques and form in ways that have never been possible. There can also be precision in practice. For example, the German tennis federation used video analysis and biometrics for years to create a programme called Point-by-Point, which allows nationally ranked players to replay any point after every competition. Using the AI algorithm, the technique of any given player can be dissected and altered for improvement. Artificial intelligence is now unleashed for even young athletes, empowering them with competitive advantages.

23.1.3. Injury Prevention and Recovery:

AI is, perhaps, returning sport to a magic-free environment and restoring some predictability in human outcomes The implementation of AI in sports medicine has already been revolutionary with regards to injury prevention and management. The potential game-changing role that AI can play in sports medicine relates to the prevention and management of injuries. Prevention can save a considerable amount of time, whilst ameliorating the consequences of accidents or injuries can bring players back to the game quicker. By examining patterns in training loads, previous injury history, biomechanics and other metrics to determine injury risk, AI can identify and even predict the likelihood of injury. Adjusting the required loads to be as challenging as possible while still reducing the risk of injury, and progressive overload can be implemented in a more effective and personalised manner. AI can also optimise the programme and progression during the rehabilitation stages, by adapting programmes to the individual's ongoing status, providing continuous and more effective feedback during recovery.

23.1.4. Mental Toughness and Cognitive Training:

Beyond physical conditioning, AI enhances mental training and readies us for tough situations. AI-supported neurofeedback and cognitive training programmes sharpen an athlete's focus, decision-making and stress tolerance – allowing them to train for and be mentally prepared for peak or pressure-packed performance.

23.1.5. Tactical and Strategic Insights:

For team sports, AI can complement existing factors to provide enhanced tactical and strategic analysis, thanks to its analysis of large sets of prior game data, to isolate activities, capabilities and weaknesses in the player's own team and their opponents. This allows game-plans to be reviewed and revised more frequently, with greater effectiveness, based on real-time inputs during competition.

23.2 Actionable Steps for Young Athletes

23.2.1. Embrace Wearable Technology:

Firstly, integrate wearable technology into your training. A variety of smartwatches, fitness trackers, and biometric devices can help track your physical activity, functional capacities, vital signs and other relevant information on your performance, health and recovery. Tap into this data: use it to set objectives, get smart feedback on your progress, and evaluate your training information to make informed decisions.

23.2.2. Leverage AI-Powered Apps and Platforms:

Use mobile apps and platforms for sports training that provide tailored training programmes, video analysis and feedback in real time. Shop around to see what suits your needs and your sport.

23.2.3. Focus on Data-Driven Training:

Secondly, be decision-responsive Make decisions about your training based on data. Take a reading from your performance data once a week, for instance, and make specific corrections to your training programme to capitalise on your strengths and correct your inherent weaknesses.

23.2.4. Incorporate Mental Training:

Just remember, it's just as important to train your brain as it is to train your body. Use the rapid advancements in AI-driven cognitive training tools in order to become more focused, make better decisions and manage stress. Try integrating visualisation and mental imagery techniques into your practice to prepare for competitive environments.

23.2.5. Work with Coaches and Experts:

Collaborate with coaches and AI sport specialists, including players in AI sports, who can help your use of AI to 'train smarter', rather than just 'train harder'. Such collaborators might assist you to select the right AI tools, explain why they're good for you, and integrate them into your overall game strategy. Experts can inform you, for example, if your workouts should focus more on endurance or strength, ensuring that your training is not just physically, but also morally, intelligent.

23.2.6. Stay Informed and Adapt:

The AI in sports space will continue to see innovation in terms of technology, best practices and applications. Keep abreast of what's going on in the industry so you're able to adapt your training routine around newer AI tools and insights. Don't be afraid to experiment.

23.3 Encouraging Continuous Learning and Adaptation

AI might be used in sports today, but becoming AI-First is an ongoing process. If young athletes want to reach their full potential, they should cultivate an ongoing willingness to learn and change. Here's what they should do.

23.3.1. Engage in Lifelong Learning:

Ensure lifelong learning is built into your athletic journey. Take workshops, courses and online Masterclasses for athletes on AI and sports science; join communities of other athletes and experts to share knowledge and experiences.

23.3.2. Experiment and Innovate:

Keep trying new things. Sometimes leaning into new AI technologies and training approaches can be as important as trying to avoid failure. By staying flexible and incorporating lessons from your failures, you'll be a much better scientist.

23.3.3. Seek Feedback and Reflect:

Get feedback from coaches, peers and AI systems. Reflect on what you're doing; reflect on your training; use that reflection to guide action and modification.

23.3.4. Adapt to Changing Conditions:

Sports are fluid. Conditions are ever-changing. New AI technology. A new competition format. Forest fires. A cat with its paws buried in your mulch. Be ready to pivot. Be agile and resilient.

23.3.5. Ethical Considerations:

As you incorporate AI into training, bear ethics in mind: respect privacy and data security; promote fair play; and recognise ways that bias may be introduced into AI systems so that use of the technology can also promote fair play, especially when considering not just player performance but also sporting integrity.

23.4 Conclusion

Although harnessing AI in sport is a complex endeavour with inevitable challenges for young individuals, it offers unique opportunities (namely through personalised training programmes and interventions, AI-driven match/game analysis, injury detection and prevention, mental training, tactical training and insights) to help athletes realise their fullest potential. Nurturing athletes along this path calls for a systemic and perpetual combination of learning, adapting and ethical considerations. So, remember, as you're exploring a career in sports, AI is not your enemy. In fact, when wielded intelligently and ethically, it is your superpower. Welcome to the future of AI-powered sports. The next big thing is here.

CHAPTER TWENTY-FOUR

Significant References

They draw on the work of people as disparate as sporting legends and seminal figures in AI and technology in sport. They form a broad base of knowledge on which to draw valuable information for this book.

24.1 Sports Personalities

1. Lionel Messi - Football
2. Serena Williams - Tennis
3. Usain Bolt - Athletics
4. Sachin Tendulkar - Cricket
5. Michael Jordan - Basketball
6. Cristiano Ronaldo - Football
7. Simone Biles - Gymnastics
8. Roger Federer - Tennis
9. Virat Kohli - Cricket
10. LeBron James - Basketball
11. Marta Vieira da Silva - Football

12. Rafael Nadal - Tennis

13. Novak Djokovic - Tennis

14. Michael Phelps – Swimming

15. Ellie Simmonds - Paralympic Swimming

24.2 AI Specialists and Innovators in Sports

16. Peter Sondergaard -

Former EVP, Research at Gartner, AI in sports analytics.

17. Daryl Morey –

President of Basketball Operations for the Philadelphia 76ers, a data analytics cheerleader in professional sports.

18. Rajiv Maheswaran -

Co-founder of Second Spectrum, AI and sports analytics

19. Mark Cuban -

Owner of Dallas Mavericks, investor in sports technology

20. Bill James -

Pioneer of sabermetrics in baseball

21. Billy Beane -

Executive Vice President of Oakland Athletics, known for Moneyball

22. Kirk Goldsberry -

NBA analyst and author, expert in sports data visualization

23. Patrick Lucey -

Chief Scientist at Stats Perform, AI in sports

24. Gillian Zucker –

President of Business Operations for the LA Clippers, use of AI to augment team operations.

25. Yuval Noah Harari -

Historian and author with insights into the future of AI

26. Cathy O'Neil –

Author of Weapons of Math Destruction (2016), on the potential ethical implications of AI in sports

27. Steve McManaman -

Former footballer and advocate for technology in sports broadcasting

28. Sundar Pichai -

CEO of Alphabet Inc., insights into AI advancements

29. Demis Hassabis -

Co-founder and CEO of DeepMind, AI and its potential in sports

30. David Epstein –

Author of 'The Sports Gene', on how genetics and technology impact sport.

24.3 Areas of Sports & Locations where AI is already being used

Here is an input that describes people and countries where Artificial Intelligence (AI) is being used to boost the performance of sportsmen and sportswomen and what kinds of sports are they using it for.

We would like writers to paraphrase this into human-sounding text while retaining quotes and citations.

Here is the paraphrased version:

People and countries: To begin, soccer and tennis are currently among the few sports that rely heavily on technology. Moreover, there are more countries that can use AI to boost their sportspeople's performance. In addition, the United Arab Emirates is significantly "surprising" by having facilities like AI soccer robots.

Artificial Intelligence: Secondly, there are two types of Artificial Intelligence - basic and advanced. Basic technologies such as microphones are very common and involve perception. Additionally, these technologies facilitate training, provide safety, and manage performance.

References and applications of AI in sports around the world and across all leagues highlight the wide-reaching use of AI in sport and how it affects not only the evolution of sports but all our lives in some manner. Looking up these individuals, countries, and specific AI applications to understand the target of each reference not only serve as good examples for readers of this book on the role of AI in future sports.

24.3.1 People and AI Use in Sports

1. Yuji Matsuzaki (Japan) - AI in Baseball

Now, I'm head of AI [artificial intelligence]. I'm helping the company using artificial intelligence to analyse baseball player performance and strategy.

2. Ben Alamar (USA) - AI in Basketball

- Head of Sports Analytics at ESPN, where he uses AI to help improve basketball performance.

3. Sam Robertson (Australia) - AI in Australian Rules Football

- Associate Professor at Victoria University, utilises AI to enhance player performance and prevent injuries in Australian Rules Football.

4. Paolo Barone (Italy) - AI in Football (Soccer)

- Data scientist at Juventus FC, implementing AI for player performance tracking and match analysis.

5. Ruth Purcell (UK) - AI in Rugby

- Performance analyst at the English Rugby Football Union, using AI to stop player injuries

6. Jeremy Poirier (Canada) - AI in Ice Hockey

- Co-founder of Softlogic, a company using AI to provide advanced analytics for ice hockey.

7. Kazuhiro Kosuge (Japan) - AI in Judo

- Professor at Tohoku University, utilizing AI for biomechanical analysis and performance improvement in Judo.

8. Michel Bruyninckx (Belgium) - AI in Youth Football Development

- Created the 'SenseBall' training programme, incorporating AI to help young footballers develop cognitive as well as motor skills.

24.3.2 Countries and AI Use in Sports

1. United States

- Baseball: Major League Baseball (MLB) sources player performance data and league and franchise strategy from AI.

- Basketball: NBA teams using AI for advanced performance tracking and predictive analytics.

2. Japan

- Baseball: NTT Data's AI solutions for player performance and strategy.

- Judo: AI-driven biomechanical analysis for training improvements.

3. Australia

- Cricket: AI used by Cricket Australia for player performance analysis and injury prevention.

- Australian Rules Football: AI applications for player tracking and performance enhancement.

4. United Kingdom

- Football/Soccer: Premier League teams using AI to analyse matches, track players and optimise performance.

- Rugby: AI-driven performance and injury management systems used by the Rugby Football Union.

5. Germany

- Football (Soccer): Bundesliga clubs leveraging AI for tactical analysis, player performance, and injury prevention.

6. Spain

Football (Soccer): Players and coaches of La Liga teams to use software that incorporates AI to better evaluate upcoming matches, scout opponents, and assess the development of players.

7. India

- Cricket: Indian Premier League (IPL) teams use this to analyse players' performance and optimise their strategy.

8. Canada

Ice Hockey: NHL teams use AI to improve players' performances by building a system that analyses games.

9. France

- Football (Soccer): League 1 teams utilizing AI for match performance and player development.

10. Italy

- Football (Soccer): Serie A clubs integrating AI for tactical and player performance analytics.

24.3.3 Specific AI Applications in Sports

1. Performance Analysis
- AI algorithms analysing player movements, strategies, and game dynamics to improve overall performance.

2. Injury Prevention
- Predictive AI models identifying injury risks and suggesting preventive measures based on player data.

3. Talent Scouting
- Systems analysing masses of data and recorded video to generate player assessments of the young.

4. Match Strategy
- AI-driven tactical analysis helping coaches develop game strategies based on opponent strengths and weaknesses.

5. Fan Engagement
- AI applications enhancing fan experiences through personalized content and interactive features.

These references and cases illustrate the multi-faceted and influential use of AI in international sports. Studying all of them helps understand the current status of AI in sports and the potential developments in the future.

SELECTED BOOKS PUBLISHED BY DR. SELVA

These books can be viewed/ bought by following the link below to the Amazon site:

https://selvasmail.com/selvasbooks

Alternatively, should you wish to view the books on your phone or tablet, you could scan the barcode below, which will also take you direct to the Amazon site.

Scan me

BOOKS ON WELLNESS & HEALTH (7 BOOKS)

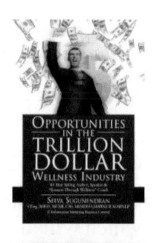

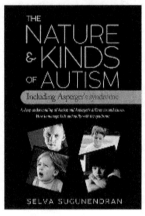

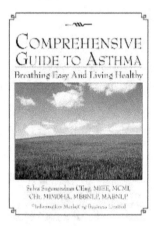

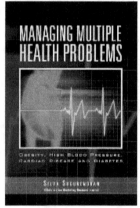

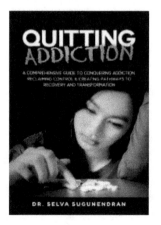

BOOKS ON ALZHEIMER'S DEMENTIA (6 BOOKS)

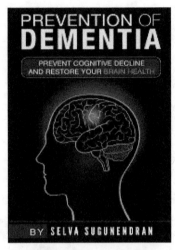

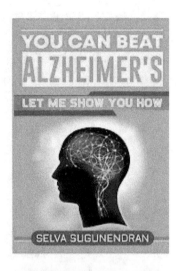

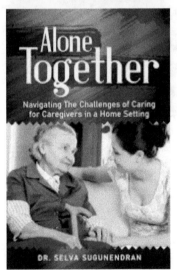

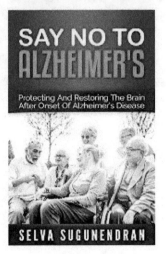

BOOKS ON SUCCESS (5 Books)

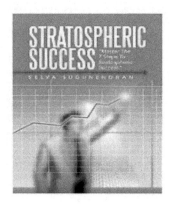

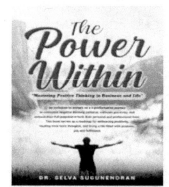

AI ROBOTICS (7 BOOKS)

AI and Its **TRAJECTORY**

Navigating the Age of Enlightenment and Addressing the Threats to Humanity

By DR. SELVA SUGUNENDRAN

SUPERHUMAN REVOLUTION

A Guide to Thriving in the Age of Advanced Intelligence

DR. Selva Sugunendran

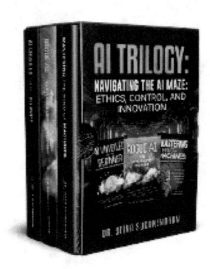

AI TRILOGY:

NAVIGATING THE AI MAZE: ETHICS, CONTROL, AND INNOVATION

CHRISTIAN BOOKS (18 BOOKS)

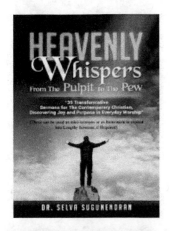

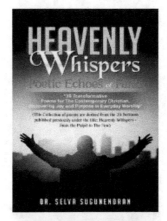

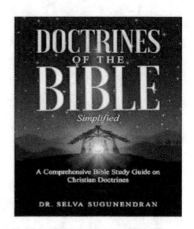

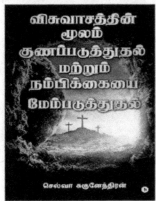

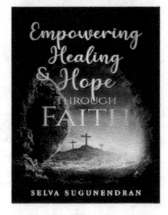

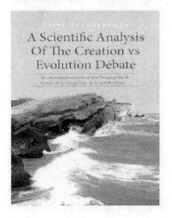

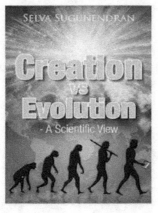

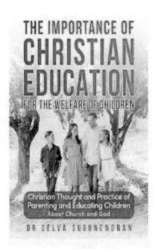

THE IMPORTANCE OF
CHRISTIAN EDUCATION
FOR THE WELFARE OF CHILDREN

Christian Thought and Practice of
Parenting and Educating Children
- About Church and God -

DR SELVA SUGUNENDRAN

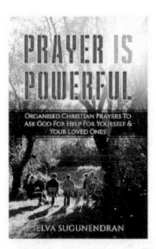

PRAYER IS POWERFUL

ORGANISED CHRISTIAN PRAYERS TO
ASK GOD FOR HELP FOR YOURSELF &
YOUR LOVED ONES

SELVA SUGUNENDRAN

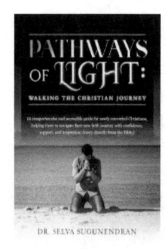

PATHWAYS OF LIGHT:
WALKING THE CHRISTIAN JOURNEY

DR. SELVA SUGUNENDRAN

A LIVE DEBATE
AMONGST 3 YOUNG SCIENTISTS
On Eight Key Areas of Evolution

SELVA SUGUNENDRAN

21 REASONS
Why Evolution Lacks Scientific Proof

SELVA SUGUNENDRAN

BIG BANG
THEORY DEMYSTIFIED

SELVA SUGUNENDRAN

THE POWER OF DIVINE
CONVERSATIONS
UNLOCKING THE SECRETS OF PRAYER

DR. SELVA SUGUNENDRAN

UNANSWERED
Prayers
- A JOURNEY OF FAITH

DR. SELVA SUGUNENDRAN

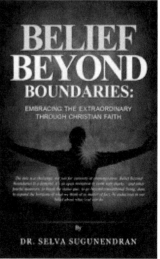

BELIEF BEYOND
BOUNDARIES:
EMBRACING THE EXTRAORDINARY
THROUGH CHRISTIAN FAITH

By
DR. SELVA SUGUNENDRAN

APPENDICES

1. WEBSITE LINKS

https://AIRoboticsForGood.com

https://MyChristianLifestyle.org

https://BlessMeLord.com

https://HealMeLord.today

https://CreationEvolutionAndScience.com

https://AIRoboticsForGood.com

https://DementiaAdvice.care

https://HowToLeadAVibrantLifeWithAlzheimers.com

2. CONTACT LINKS:

The Author Email: Selva@MyChristianLifestyle.org

All Books by Author Available on Amazon:

https://selvasmail.com/selvasbooks